D0065318

PHILIPPIANS

PHILIPPIANS

A Biblical Study

JOYCE MEYER

Faith
Words

NEW YORK • NASHVILLE

FaithWords
Hachette Book Group
1290 Avenue of the Americas, New York, NY 10104
faithwords.com
twitter.com/faithwords

First Edition: March 2021

FaithWords is a division of Hachette Book Group, Inc. The FaithWords name and logo are trademarks of Hachette Book Group, Inc.

The publisher is not responsible for websites (or their content) that are not owned by the publisher.

The Hachette Speakers Bureau provides a wide range of authors for speaking events. To find out more, go to www.hachettespeakersbureau.com or call (866) 376-6591.

Library of Congress Cataloging-in-Publication Data has been applied for.

ISBNs: 978-1-5460-2618-1 (hardcover), 978-1-5460-2616-7 (ebook)

Printed in the United States of America

LSC-C

Printing 1, 2021

CONTENTS

HOW TO STUDY THIS BOOK

I would like to suggest that you take your time studying this book. Don't just skim over the book so you can finish it quickly, but take your time not only reading but also pondering what you read. Stop at places that are important to you, and think about how they apply to you personally and whether or not you need to make changes in your life in order to walk more fully in God's will.

I encourage you to answer the questions provided for you at various points in this study, because they will help you recognize areas in which you need to grow.

I also want to suggest that you take the time to look up the Scripture references that appear throughout the book. Space does not permit us to print out each verse in full, but you can open your Bible to the references mentioned and read the Scripture passages for yourself. The effort you put into doing this will enhance your overall experience and will allow you to truly absorb the truths of God's Word.

Remember that studying is different than simply reading. When we read, we take in information, but when we study, the information becomes revelation to us—it becomes part of us and transforms our lives and behavior in deeper ways than a quick reading does.

ABOUT PHILIPPIANS

Author: *Paul*
Date: *Around AD 61*
Audience: *Christians in the city of Philippi*

The apostle Paul's letter to the Philippians is considered "the epistle of joy," and Paul mentions joy approximately thirteen times in the four chapters of this book of the Bible, sometimes more, depending on the translation we read. Although Jesus was "a man of suffering, and familiar with pain" (Isaiah 53:3), He also possessed a deep joy beyond anything the world can offer. As He faced a terrible death on Calvary, Jesus spoke to His disciples, saying, "I have told you this so that my joy may be in you and that your joy may be complete" (John 15:11). Jesus came to Earth so that we might "have and enjoy life, and have it in abundance [to the full, till it overflows]" (John 10:10 AMP). God wants us to be happy and joyful. Paul definitely understood that and helps us understand and experience this truth through his warm and personal letter to the believers at Philippi.

Paul wrote this epistle while he was held captive in a Roman prison. Even under the difficult circumstances of incarceration, he still found joy! What was his secret? I believe it was that he learned to think according to God's Word. He mentions the mind and/or functions of the mind at least ten times in this letter, so we can see that joy is connected to our thoughts and mindsets. If we choose to live with a positive perspective, even the worst circumstances cannot steal our joy.

Paul visited Philippi for the first time during his second missionary journey, which took place around AD 52. If Paul was approximately twenty years old when his Damascus Road experience took place—the dramatic encounter in which Jesus appeared to him and radically changed his life (you can read about it in Acts 9)—he would have been at least seventy years old when he wrote this letter. Yet he was still determined to do God's will, which for him was to preach the gospel.

Paul strategically chose the cities to which he took the gospel. He selected places that were important in themselves but also major hubs for entire geographic areas. Philippi was one of these cities, and if we understand its significance, we see that Paul's choice to preach and minister in such an influential place is not surprising. Philippi was important because it had been known historically as a city of rich gold and silver mines, though the mines had been exhausted by the time of Paul's ministry.

In 368 BC, King Philip II of Macedonia, the father of

Alexander the Great, founded this city, and it was named after him. In 42 BC, after the assassination of Julius Caesar, Philippi was the site of a major battle. In that contest, an army under the command of Mark Antony and Octavian defeated the forces of Brutus and Cassius, who had led the effort to kill Caesar, and thereby determined the future of the Roman Empire.

In Paul's day, Roman colonies were scattered throughout the vast Roman Empire, and they helped keep the empire at peace. The well-known Roman Road system was constructed for travel among these colonies.

By the time Paul visited Philippi, the city had been raised to the status of a Roman colony, and the people who lived there were either Jews or Roman citizens. Paul was both. His being a Roman citizen and a Jew allowed him to preach to both Jews and Romans. It also afforded him special protection on several occasions as he went about preaching the gospel.

Paul's writing reveals that he formed close ties with the believers at Philippi and enjoyed an intimate friendship with them. His bond with them was greater than his bond with any other church. In Philippians 4:1, he affirms his special relationship with the Philippians, calling them his "joy and crown."

At the time Paul wrote Philippians, most aspects of daily life in Philippi were strongly influenced by Roman culture. Citizens spoke Latin, the language of the Roman Empire. People wore Roman clothing styles, and a strong Roman military presence was noticeable around the city. The citizens of Philippi also had a robust sense of cultural pride in their identity as subjects of the Roman Empire and aggressively resisted non-Roman cultural influences.

In Philippi, the citizens who staunchly aligned with Rome persecuted the Christians in their midst, accusing them of trying to institute laws and customs that did not align with those of Rome. The primary purpose for which Paul wrote this letter was to encourage the Philippian believers during this time of hardship. Paul's Roman citizenship did help him during this time of difficulty for Christians, but not enough for him to avoid all persecution and illegal imprisonment.

Acts 16 includes a story about Paul's visit to Philippi, which involved three main characters—each of them very different. We meet Lydia, a female merchant from Asia referred to as "a dealer in purple cloth" and "a worshiper of God" (Acts 16:14). We also read about a slave girl, whose owners viewed her—as other slaves of the day were viewed—not as a person but as a tool to be used in the hands of her master, who, in this case, used her to tell fortunes. And we are introduced to a jailer, who was a Roman citizen. As we can see from the variety of personalities and backgrounds represented in Acts 16, Paul encountered many segments of Philippian society, from the highest to the lowest.

It also is about two women and one man with vastly dissimilar backgrounds. This chapter of the New Testament shows that Jesus offers an all-inclusive faith to everyone, and Paul's ministry reached different types of people as well.

Philippians is one of my favorite epistles because it not only encouraged believers in the early church but also addresses a wide variety of situations that we encounter in our lives today—such as conducting ourselves in a manner worthy of the gospel (Philippians 1:27); overcoming selfishness (Philippians 2:3–4); resisting the temptation to complain and argue (Philippians 2:14); letting go of the past and looking toward the future (Philippians 3:13); rejoicing in the Lord, no matter what (Philippians 4:4); staying at peace instead of living in anxiety (Philippians 4:6–7); godly thinking (Philippians 4:8); and trusting God to meet our needs (Philippians 4:19)—and helps us know how to handle them properly. I am sure you will be enriched by your study of Philippians, and I pray that this book helps you on your journey of spiritual growth.

Key Truths in Philippians

- We can be confident that God has begun a good work in us and that He will complete it (Philippians 1:6).
- Jesus laid aside His rights and privileges and took on human flesh, feeling sorrow, pain, and the weight of our sin. He did this in obedience to His Father so that we might ultimately be reconciled to Him (Philippians 2:5–8).
- Salvation is a gift from God, and it changes us completely. Once we receive it in our hearts, we are to demonstrate it in our lives (Philippians 2:12).
- We may be tempted to place our confidence in all kinds of things, such as our abilities or our resources,

but our confidence and trust should be in Christ
alone (Philippians 3:3).

- God puts people into our lives as examples and role
models to help us grow in faith. Paul provided this
kind of example to the Philippians (Philippians 3:17).
- As Christians, joy should be one of the hallmarks of
our lives (Philippians 4:4).
- We do not have to think whatever thoughts come
into our minds. We can choose our thoughts
(Philippians 4:8).

CHAPTER 1

PAUL'S POWERFUL OPENING WORDS TO THE PHILIPPIANS

A Greeting to Friends

Philippians 1:1–2

Paul and Timothy, servants of Christ Jesus, to all God's holy people in Christ Jesus at Philippi, together with the overseers and deacons: Grace and peace to you from God our Father and the Lord Jesus Christ.

It is noticeable, and I think commendable, that in many of his letters Paul links himself with younger, less experienced fellow laborers. He makes mention of the young man who is traveling with him, Timothy, and writes of him when he addresses this letter to the church leaders, in addition to all the believers at Philippi. Paul did for Timothy what more mature Christians should do for younger believers today. He was mentoring him in the ministry, teaching him not only by word but also by living closely with him, enabling him to see his consistent example. Paul was a model for other teachers and ministers, and we can learn from his example (Philippians 3:17).

The people we choose as friends and mentors are extremely important, because we become like those with whom we spend our time. I encourage you to find people who model characteristics and qualities you would like to develop in yourself and spend time with them. Watch how they handle various situations in life, and let them be a pattern of godly behavior for you. If the Lord leads you to do so, ask them if they are willing to mentor you by meeting with you on a regular basis for the purpose of teaching you and providing a measure of accountability for you.

Maintaining a high level of generosity in my life is important to me, so I choose generous people with whom to spend my time. If I spent my time with stingy and greedy people, I might drift in their direction, and I don't want to do that. I also don't want to spend time with people who murmur and complain or gossip and criticize. I want to be a positive person and an encourager, so I choose to spend the majority of my time with people who model optimism and encouragement.

Personal Reflection

Who do you know who would be a good mentor for you? What qualities does this person have that you would like to incorporate into your life or in which you would like to grow?

_____

_____

_____

_____

_____

I have heard many stories from people who have been deeply disappointed by church leaders who preached and taught godly behavior but did not live according to their teachings. Some of those disillusioned people left the church and returned only after years of encouragement, and some never came back. As leaders in the church, we have a great responsibility to live what we teach, realizing that people look to us not only to exemplify proper behavior but also to see if we are truly doing what we tell others to do. This is important for Christian business leaders, parents, and teachers, as well as for every believer.

People who tell others how to behave while failing to behave that way in their own lives are called hypocrites. Bible students know that Jesus harshly rebukes hypocritical people. Matthew 23:27–28 includes a strong reprimand from Jesus to religious people who were hypocrites, and He tells them they are like whitewashed tombs filled with dead men's bones. They tell others what to do but do not do it themselves.

In Paul's letter to Titus, whom he called his "true son," he writes, "In everything set them an example by doing what is good. In your teaching show integrity, seriousness and soundness of speech that cannot be condemned, so that those who oppose you may be ashamed because they have nothing bad to say about us" (Titus 1:4; 2:7–8). This reminds me of a familiar anonymous quotation: "Preach at all times. When necessary, use words." In other words, we are to let our lives be like living sermons, demonstrating through our words and actions our faith and our love for God and for other people.

Servants to All

In Philippians 1, Paul and Timothy claim no official title except "servants of Christ Jesus." They considered themselves purchased by Christ with no rights to their own lives. They had renounced everything except the will of God. To serve God means to serve others, but some people don't understand that. To say that we serve God sounds very spiritual, but to serve people because of our love for God is the proof of being a servant.

The Bible gives us an account of Jesus wrapping a servant's towel around Himself after dinner and washing the disciples' feet (John 13:2–5). Jesus tells the disciples that they are to do what they see Him do. He says, "You call me 'Teacher' and 'Lord,' and rightly so, for that is what I am. Now that I, your Lord and Teacher, have washed your feet, you also should wash one another's feet. I have set you an example that you should do as I have done for you" (John 13:13–15). Being a true servant to God and to others is the character trait of a great man or woman of God. When the disciples asked Jesus who was the greatest among them, He replied that the greatest of all is the servant of all (Matthew 20:25–26).

In the Old Testament, prophets are usually referred to as servants of God, as are great men of faith, such as Moses and David. I wonder how many of us consider greatness to consist of serving others. I would venture to say that if we took the world's view of serving people, rather than the biblical view, we would think that greatness means being served, not being servants. I have found quite a few of the principles regarding the Kingdom of God to be the opposite of what the world would expect. For example, the world would urge us to exact revenge on our enemies, but Jesus teaches us to forgive, pray for, and bless them (Luke 6:27–28). The very reason life doesn't work without God in it is that He is the One with all the right answers about how to live and behave, even if some of them don't seem to fit into our logical thinking.

I am the president of a ministry and therefore the highest official of that organization, but I consistently make an effort never to think of myself as above any of the others who serve along with me. We are a team, and it is important for each one to do his or her part. I think this would be a good time for each of us to set aside a little time and examine our own life and attitudes and see how we rate when it comes to serving others as a service to God.

Personal Reflection

Think about your life and your attitude toward serving others. Do you serve people as a way of serving God? In what ways do you—or could you—make a priority of serving others?

_____

_____

_____

_____

_____

Grace and Peace

Paul opens many of his letters with the same greeting he uses in Philippians: "Grace and peace to you." I must admit that I read the Bible for years without giving any thought to the importance of these opening words. But I now realize how valuable and beautiful they are. Grace is God's favor and power freely given to those who don't deserve it. Grace opens the door for us to know God and therefore be happy. We are saved by grace and can do nothing without it. In addition, we all want and need peace. A life without peace is a miserable life, but we cannot have it without an understanding of grace.

Grace accomplishes with ease, through us, what we could never do with any amount of our own effort and struggle. It is by God's grace through faith that we are saved, and we should live each day the same way (Ephesians 2:8). In our dealings with others, we should learn to extend grace as God does to us. More mercy and less criticism would heal a lot of wounded relationships.

God's Word teaches us to live in peace and also to be peacemakers (1 Peter 3:11). Jesus Himself said in Matthew 5:9: "Blessed are the peacemakers, for they will be called children of God." Being a person who works toward maintaining peace at all times requires a great deal of humility. Human nature causes us to want to have the last word in any kind of disagreement and to want to be right. However, in order to keep peace, at times we will need to give up any "right" we feel that we have to be right and refuse to argue simply for the sake of expressing an opinion that no one even wants to hear.

My son once said, "Being right is highly overrated." After many years of defending my opinions and offering them too frequently, which often led to arguments and strife, I finally realized that if I needed others to recognize that I was right, God could easily take care of that. I also learned that where humility is present, appearing to be wrong doesn't bother us at all.

I pray that God's grace and peace would be upon you all the time, and that God would give you a receptive heart to receive and live in them.

Personal Reflection

What can you do to receive God's grace and peace on a deeper level in your life?

_____

_____

_____

_____

_____

_____

CHAPTER 2

HOW TO DEVELOP AND MAINTAIN GODLY RELATIONSHIPS

Thanksgiving and Prayer
Philippians 1:3–5

I thank my God every time I remember you. In all my prayers for all of you, I always pray with joy because of your partnership in the gospel from the first day until now.

Paul begins this section by letting his readers know that every time he thinks about them, he thanks God for them. Paul had a grateful heart, and that is beautiful to God. The psalmist says that we enter His gates "with thanksgiving" (Psalm 100:4), which helps us understand that a grateful heart is a prerequisite to enjoying God's presence. Many scriptures throughout the Bible instruct us to be thankful and give thanks to the Lord.

Paul also lets the Philippians know that it is his joy to pray for them all. Paul had a closer relationship to the Philippian church than to any others, and I think these verses show us why. The believers at Philippi became partners in Paul's ministry from the first day they heard the gospel and were still supporting him when he wrote this letter. Later in our study of Philippians, we will find Paul stating that they were the only church to enter into true partnership with him. Others gave offerings at times, but only the Philippians are referred to as partners in his ministry.

Paul diligently avoided asking for financial support from
those to whom he ministered and instead worked to make
his own living. He normally refused to ask people to help him
because he did not want anyone to discredit him as a false
apostle merely looking for monetary gain. Apparently, though,
the Philippians so strongly insisted that they be allowed to
partner financially with Paul that he ultimately yielded to their
request.

Paul understood the importance and benefits of giving to
the work of the ministry. We know this because he encourages
the Corinthians to give and teaches them about the power
of giving (2 Corinthians 8:7, 11; 9:6–11). He writes that they
will reap as they have sown and that they should be cheerful
givers. He also promises they will be enriched in every way
through their generosity (2 Corinthians 9:11). Teaching people
to give to the Lord's work and to those in need is important.
It prevents us from being greedy and selfish while opening a
door of blessing for us and for those to whom we give.

In John 13:8, when Jesus washes His disciples' feet, Peter
first refuses to let Him wash his feet. He states that he is
the one who needs to wash his Master's feet. Jesus replies,
"Unless I wash you, you have no part with me." Jesus seems
to be indicating that the only way to have a real relationship
is to both give and receive from one another.

Many people are comfortable giving to others, but giving to
them is very difficult. They know how to give graciously, but
not how to receive graciously. Their usual reply is, "I'm fine,
I don't need anything," but that statement may be birthed

either in pride or in such a poor self-image that they believe they don't deserve anything. We should give graciously and receive graciously as well.

Personal Reflection

Are you a giving person, eager to bless others? Do you also allow others the joy of giving to you by receiving their blessings graciously?

_____

_____

_____

_____

_____

_____

Healthy Relationships

We can learn a lot about healthy relationships from Paul's relationship with the Philippians. One lesson I have learned about relationships is that a one-sided relationship is not a healthy one. Good relationships require participation with one another, each contributing something to it. If one person does all the giving while the other does all the taking, the relationship soon declines into something unhappy, unfulfilling, and unhealthy for the one who gives and never receives. If you are in any relationships like this, I suggest that you pray and ask God to intervene and put it on the heart of your co-worker, relative, or friend to do their part in giving as well as receiving.

I prayed this prayer recently and was astounded at how quickly things turned around in the relationship I was praying about. Prayer invites God to work in our lives and should be our first step in dealing with any situation. I am involved with someone I compliment often, especially regarding her work effort. Several years into the relationship, I started noticing that she rarely ever complimented me on anything I had done. I asked God to change the situation, and almost immediately she began complimenting me quite regularly. The power of simple, sincere prayer is amazing.

Let me encourage you not ever to say, "Well, I guess there is nothing left to do but pray." Praying is always the first thing we should do, not the last. Prayer invites God to help us, and without His help we become quickly worn out from fleshly efforts, trying to make something happen that only God can accomplish. Only He can change a person's heart, and in this instance He did so very quickly.

I have a great relationship with a woman who owns a clothing boutique where I have purchased most of my clothing for approximately thirty-five years. I give her money through purchasing, and she gives me great service. We are also friends beyond the buying and selling relationship. We have lunch together, she calls when she needs prayer, and I can always count on her to get me what I need to wear for any event I am attending. It is not a one-sided relationship. This year on my birthday she gave me a very generous gift certificate to a spa, and she said she just wanted to do something special for me so I would know how much I mean to her.

These activities—such as sharing meals together or giving and receiving gifts and others—are the glue that holds good relationships together. An exchange between friends does not need to be financial. It can take many forms. All we need to do is ask God to show us what someone else needs and listen. He may let us know by giving us a thought or an idea, but often the person will soon tell us without even intending to do so what they need or would like. When we are ready to be givers as well as receivers, our relationships will remain healthy.

I have also had many one-sided relationships in which I was continually asked to do favors for people, yet they never did anything for me. I realize that Jesus says we should give to others without expecting anything in return (Luke 6:35). But I believe that refers more to developing an attitude of blessing and generosity than to thinking we should never receive anything.

I once had a strong desire to be content and not want anything for myself. Because of that, I continued to give into the lives of several people who never gave back even a word of encouragement to me. One day I realized that these relationships were draining to me, and that I was enabling these people to continue in selfish lifestyles. I prayed diligently and felt that God showed me that these relationships were unhealthy. He had used me to give to people, but since they continued to give nothing in return, they were disrespecting the relationship and taking advantage of me. I came to understand that allowing that unhealthy pattern to continue would not be good for them. I am always happy to give to anyone to whom God desires me to give, but I am also willing to say no to them if He leads me to do so. I am no longer in unhealthy, draining relationships.

We should choose our friends wisely, and I look for people with whom to partner in life and ministry. I look for people who are there for me when I have a need, just as they expect me to be available for them. I have many such people in my life—people who receive from me or from the ministry but who are also givers in many different ways. I once spoke at a man's church upon request, and since that time he has not failed to send me occasional gifts. It is not the item that is important, but the fact that he is still in some way saying, "Thank you, Joyce, for coming to help my church."

I strongly suggest that we examine all of our relationships and discern what types of relationships they are. There may be seasons when God will guide us to be in a relationship in which we do all the giving. He may be trying to use us as examples of how to be a good friend, but if other people never learn the lessons, God will release us from the responsibility. We should always obey God without expecting anything in return, but God would never function in that way with us. Throughout His Word, He promises to reward those who are obedient and faithful to Him. We don't obey God to get a reward, but because we love Him; however, when we give with right hearts, His blessings will chase us.

Personal Reflection

Think about your relationships. Which ones are healthy and include both giving and receiving? Which ones do you need to pray about and reconsider because you are giving too much?

_____

_____

_____

_____

_____

_____

God Finishes What He Begins

Philippians 1:6–8

Being confident of this, that he who began a good work in you will carry it on to completion until the day of Christ Jesus. It is right for me to feel this way about all of you, since I have you in my heart and, whether I am in chains or defending and confirming the gospel, all of you share in God's grace with me. God can testify how I long for all of you with the affection of Christ Jesus.

In Philippians 1:6, Paul tells us that we can be confident that God, who has begun a good work in us, "will carry it on to completion until the day of Christ Jesus," meaning the day when Christ returns to take us home to heaven. For many years after I received grace for salvation, I behaved as though I had to finish the work God had begun. I tried very hard, with a great deal of frustration and struggle, to be everything God wanted me to be, but I kept failing. My failure was due to trying to change myself by my own effort without asking for God's help or leaning and relying on Him. I'm thankful that I finally know I can do nothing without Christ (John 15:5).

This promise in Philippians 1:6 is a great encouragement to most people. Anyone who loves God will want to please

Him and to be and do all He desires, but we soon discover
that when a good desire fills our heart, evil always comes to
block the path to success. We need God's help in everything
we do, and the best way to get it is to ask for it! We have not
because we ask not (James 4:2).

Paul Prays for the Philippians

Philippians 1:9–11

And this is my prayer: that your love may abound more and more in knowledge and depth of insight, so that you may be able to discern what is best and may be pure and blameless for the day of Christ, filled with the fruit of righteousness that comes through Jesus Christ—to the glory and praise of God.

Just as all of Paul's letters are written for us today, as well as for his primary audience during his lifetime, so are his prayers. I have learned many lessons about right and wrong ways to pray for people by studying Paul's prayers for the churches to whom he wrote. When I began to study them, I noticed right away that he does not ask God to deliver them from their circumstances, but to give them the ability to endure their circumstances with good temper (Colossians 3:12 AMP). Rather than asking for temporal benefits, Paul prays for things that would help the people spiritually.

In Philippians 1:9–11, he prays that their "love may abound more and more in knowledge and depth of insight" and that they would be able to discern the most excellent things and be "filled with the fruit of righteousness that comes through Jesus Christ." If we take even a few minutes to think about what Paul prays, we will realize the infinite value of his prayers. For example, he prays for the Philippian believers to be strong spiritually, and if we are strong enough spiritually, we can endure whatever comes and remain steadfast in our faith and continue being good examples of godly behavior.

Studying Paul's prayers helped me realize that I prayed too much about the circumstances that I felt needed to improve and not enough about the spiritual blessings and insights that would lift me to resurrection life in Christ, where I could live above my circumstances. We all have unpleasant and difficult circumstances, but we don't have to let them control our behavior. I also realized that I did not pray nearly enough about my spiritual growth, and I prayed too much about things that I wanted or needed or about situations I wanted God to solve or remove from my life. It is certainly not wrong to ask God to help us concerning painful circumstances, but it is more important that we pray to be strengthened with all might and power in our inner being, and be filled with the fullness of God (Ephesians 3:16–19).

Personal Reflection

In what areas could you pray less about your circumstances and more about your spiritual life?

_____

_____

_____

_____

_____

_____

_____

Paul prays for the Philippians to abound in love, to have depth of spiritual insight, and to be "filled with the fruit of righteousness." This reminds me that we should guard against becoming complacent. Complacency is dangerous because it is only one step away from decline. If a person aspires to be a world-renowned musician, no matter how good she may be now, if she becomes complacent about practicing her instrument, her skill will soon begin to decline.

The same thing happens to us spiritually if we become complacent about spiritual growth. To abound means to exist in large amounts, to be packed with, to overflow, and to be crowded or full of. Let us always seek to grow more and more in every spiritual aspect of our lives. Let us desire to be like Jesus in all our ways.

Paul also prays that the Philippians would be excellent. I first learned Philippians 1:10 this way: "So that you may surely learn to sense what is vital, and approve and prize what is *excellent* and of real value" (AMPC, emphasis mine). We should never become complacent once we reach the "good enough" stage. We may think, *I'm doing all right. I'm certainly doing as well as other people I know.* We are not called to "good enough," but to press on to excellence in all areas of our lives.

How do excellent people behave? They are on time for appointments, they get to work on time, they don't leave messes for others to clean up, and they don't park in handicapped parking spaces if they are not handicapped. These people even replace the toilet paper when they use the last of it. They put their grocery carts back into the spaces marked for carts, and they respect the signs that say, "Please return your cart." If excellent people are not charged enough for an item they purchase, they will return to the store and ask the clerk to correct the mistake. They treat people with excellence. In essence, they try to do what Jesus would do in every situation they face.

Our first response to this kind of description of excellent people may prompt the thought or statement "These are little things that don't make much difference." But God sees everything, and nothing is hidden from His sight. If we are truly living for God, we should want to please Him in every "little" thing. Jesus says that if we are faithful in little things, He will make us rulers over much (Matthew 25:23). These little things in life may be situations no one will notice except God, but pleasing God is supposed to be our goal. Let's live as though He is always watching us, because He is.

CHAPTER 3

──◦──

THE POWER OF JOY AND THE SIMPLICITY OF THE GOSPEL

God Works All Things Out for Good
Philippians 1:12–17

Now I want you to know, brothers and sisters, that what has happened to me has actually served to advance the gospel. As a result, it has become clear throughout the whole palace guard and to everyone else that I am in chains for Christ. And because of my chains, most of the brothers and sisters have become confident in the Lord and dare all the more to proclaim the gospel without fear. It is true that some preach Christ out of envy and rivalry, but others out of goodwill. The latter do so out of love, knowing that I am put here for the defense of the gospel. The former preach Christ out of selfish ambition, not sincerely, supposing that they can stir up trouble for me while I am in chains.

Paul's good attitude in the midst of suffering in prison gave other Christians more boldness than they ever had previously to speak God's Word. In Philippians 1:12–17, Paul once again shows us how important prayer is when he says that his situation will turn out well through their prayers and through the Spirit of Christ. Paul also says this will happen according to his eager expectation and hope (v. 20). He believes his imprisonment will not bring him shame, but joy.

I want to stress that the people prayed, and Paul expected God to do something good. Hope is the expectation that something good will happen. I believe we often pray for God to do something positive, but we do not aggressively expect Him to do it. When we have hope, we can never be defeated, and according to Peter we are born again into an ever-living hope (1 Peter 1:3 AMP).

Hope is the anchor of our souls (Hebrews 6:19). Let's think about that. An anchor on a boat keeps the vessel in the right place even during a raging storm. Hope does the same for us. When storms come and our feelings threaten to dictate our future, if we are anchored to hope, we will remain steadfast rather than drift off in the wrong direction.

Paul had a secret that made him bold and strong. That secret is revealed in Philippians 1:20, and it was his confidence that whether he lived or died, he belonged to Christ. Paul didn't really care if he lived or died, as long as it glorified God. Paul felt that he had nothing to lose and everything to gain if he died, and so it was difficult to frighten him, no matter how severe the threat.

Just imagine how free we would be—how bold and courageous—if we had absolutely no fear of death or harm. If we are stewards for God of all things and owners of none, then we cannot fear loss. Paul writes: "However, I consider my life worth nothing to me; my only aim is to finish the race and complete the task the Lord Jesus has given me—the task of testifying to the good news of God's grace" (Acts 20:24).

The Power of the Simple Gospel

Paul was the preeminent teacher of his day, and he taught on a wide variety of subjects. Yet to the very end of his life, he was filled with zeal for teaching the power of the simple gospel. It is always a sign of spiritual decline when people's hearts have little or no interest in the simple preaching of salvation by grace through faith (Ephesians 2:8). As we grow as Christians, we may feel that we need to go on to deeper understanding and truths. This longing for growth is natural and pleasing to God. While we always want to be learning and growing, however, our first love should remain the simple gospel of salvation through Christ.

I wonder about church leaders today. Are we more interested in last Sunday's attendance numbers than in how many people received the simplicity and power of the gospel message and gave their lives to Christ? The enemy always tries to draw us away from the power of the simple gospel, and he attempted to do this to Paul. Paul's imprisonment could have hindered his work on behalf of the gospel, and that's what the enemy desired. But it actually had the opposite effect. Paul's faith became apparent even to those of Caesar's household and to all others, and they realized that Paul's bonds were for Christ's sake.

In Philippians 1:13, we read that the guards around Paul's prison cell heard the glorious gospel preached. We also know from Acts 16:29–33 that prison guards and their families believed and accepted the gospel message when Paul spoke of it while in jail. Paul was confident that God could and would bring good of any bad circumstance. I am sure you have heard the phrase *no pain, no gain*, but sometimes our pain is for someone else's gain. Paul suffered, and others were saved.

Even though Paul wrote to the Philippians while in prison, he continually speaks of his joy. I have stood in the cell where Paul was held, and it had a dirt floor and walls and was so small that I doubt he could have slept without curling into a ball. I have read that the town sewage ran through the place where Paul was kept, yet in the midst of all that, he had joy. I can tell you that he is way ahead of me on the "keep your joy" scale!

During Paul's time in prison, some people who had been jealous of him went about preaching. Although he could not rejoice in their actions because he felt they were only preaching out of envy, he focused on the fact that the gospel was being preached even if the motives were impure. He also rejoiced in the actions of the many who had been emboldened to preach the gospel through his example.

Like Paul, we can choose to focus on things that bring us joy rather than things that steal it. Paul refused to let even the most challenging of circumstances destroy his joy, and we can learn a great deal from his example. We can always find something to rejoice about if we simply look for it.

Personal Reflection

How is the enemy trying to steal your joy right now, and how can you defeat his plans? What can you rejoice in today?

_____

_____

_____

_____

_____

_____

Joy Is Our Strength

Philippians 1:18–20

But what does it matter? The important thing is that in every way, whether from false motives or true, Christ is preached. And because of this I rejoice. Yes, and I will continue to rejoice, for I know that through your prayers and God's provision of the Spirit of Jesus Christ what has happened to me will turn out for my deliverance. I eagerly expect and hope that I will in no way be ashamed, but will have sufficient courage so that now as always Christ will be exalted in my body, whether by life or by death.

Paul writes in Philippians 1:18 about rejoicing as long as Christ is being preached. In the Old Testament, Nehemiah writes about joy. He finds the people weeping and mourning and quickly tells them to stop being sad because the joy of the Lord is their strength (Nehemiah 8:10). Many of us have heard that scripture over and over, but I wonder if any of us realize its deep meaning. Joy gives us strength. We all need strength, and, I might add, we need more and more of it! Christ is our strength (Philippians 4:13), and He came that we might have joy (John 10:10). If we look at these two scriptures together, we can easily see that joy and strength go together.

Because we find strength in the joy of the Lord, the enemy

often tries to steal our joy. I have a very special ring that was given to me. After a visit to a spa, I managed to get home without it and thought it was lost. Everyone searched, but no ring. I had to decide how to respond. I called it what it was: a thing. It was a very nice thing, but still just a thing, and I knew I would not be able to take it with me when God calls me from this earthly dwelling to my heavenly home. We bring nothing into the world, and we can take nothing out of it (1 Timothy 6:7). Although I had moments when I missed the ring and felt a bit sad that it was gone, I refused to lose my joy over the lost piece of jewelry. Several months later, my daughter, who had gone to the spa with me, found it in her purse, where I had put it accidently. That loss was a test for me, but in the end, God gave the ring back to me, perhaps because I had been willing to joyfully let it go.

I urge you to strive to keep your joy no matter what is going on in your life. If you lose your joy, you lose your strength. Depression has been proven to steal physical strength, but laughter and joy are very good for our health. Even the Bible says, "A cheerful heart is good medicine" (Proverbs 17:22).

Joy can be anything from extreme hilarity to a calm delight. Joy doesn't necessarily laugh all day long and skip through life humming a song. It may simply be a steadfast, determined, calm, and delightful attitude.

The primary theme of Philippians is joy, and I hope this study will cause your joy to increase. Laugh more often, smile even if you are by yourself, and be delighted that you are God's beloved and that your future is secure in Him.

Personal Reflection

Have you experienced the strength that comes from the joy of the Lord? Or have you seen someone else who is joyful and strong in Him in the midst of loss or difficulty? Is there anything you could do to increase your level of joy?

_____

_____

_____

_____

_____

CHAPTER 4

SURRENDER, STANDING FIRM, AND LIKE-MINDEDNESS

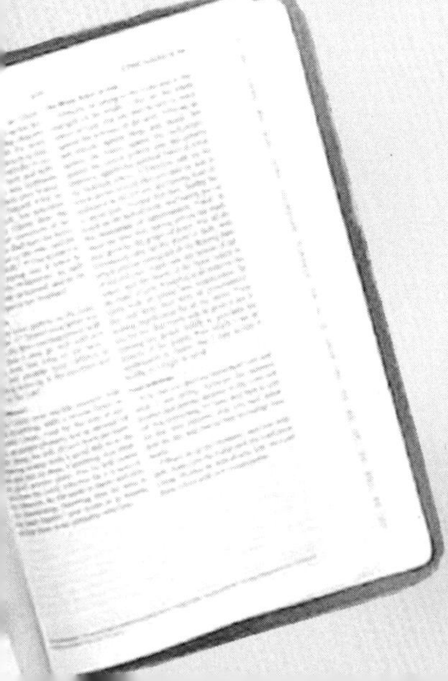

A Surrendered Will

Philippians 1:21–26

For to me, to live is Christ and to die is gain. If I am to go on living in the body, this will mean fruitful labor for me. Yet what shall I choose? I do not know! I am torn between the two: I desire to depart and be with Christ, which is better by far; but it is more necessary for you that I remain in the body. Convinced of this, I know that I will remain, and I will continue with all of you for your progress and joy in the faith, so that through my being with you again your boasting in Christ Jesus will abound on account of me.

In Philippians 1:21–26, we can clearly see that Paul didn't fear death, but seemed to prefer it. He knew that when he died and left the earthly realm, he would instantly be at home with the Lord. Only a person who has surrendered his or her will to God's will can have the attitude Paul displayed. If Paul lived, it was for Christ, and if he died, it was for Christ. It didn't matter to him whether he lived or died, as long as he could serve Jesus through it.

The will—our power to choose—is the most difficult aspect of our being to conquer and surrender to God. We begin exerting our will as infants, and it seems we never stop. We want what we don't have and resist the things we have but don't want. We want to have control over not only our own lives but, in many instances, over the lives of others, too. It seems that we love any kind of control except self-control, which is what God wants us to exercise. He has given us the fruit of self-control (Galatians 5:22–23).

A will surrendered to God—a conscious decision to do what God wants us to do, not what our fleshly nature wants us to do—is what He desires, and it always leads to joy, joy, and more joy. Paul had surrendered his will to God, and that can be easily seen in his attitude toward whether he lived or died. He said he would rather go to heaven and be with the Lord, but he felt the more beneficial choice was for him to remain and continue his ministry. He was going to be happy either way because he trusted God's plan more than his own.

Personal Reflection

Have you surrendered to God's will in your life?

_____

_____

_____

_____

_____

_____

Living Sacrifices

As I mentioned earlier, Paul would have preferred to go to heaven to be with Jesus than to stay on earth, but he wanted to stay in order to continue to minister to people. I view this as a sacrifice he made to God. When Paul writes, "For to me, to live is Christ and to die is gain," he is making a statement that only a fully surrendered person could make.

An unsaved businessperson might say, "For me, to live is money." Or an actress or singer who is not serving God might say, "For me, to live is fame." But as Christians, we should continue growing spiritually until we can say with Paul, "For me, to live is Christ." Paul only cared about God's will; nothing else held any power over him.

Paul certainly understood the principle of sacrificing and surrendering everything to God, and he instructs us to do just that in his letter to the Romans: "Therefore, I urge you, brothers and sisters, in view of God's mercy, to offer your bodies as a living sacrifice, holy and pleasing to God—this is your true and proper worship" (Romans 12:1).

Think about your body for a moment. Paul's instruction to offer ourselves as living sacrifices includes our minds, our wills, our emotions, and our physical bodies. The Amplified Bible, Classic Edition says that we should offer our bodies and our "faculties" to God as a living sacrifice. This means God wants to use our words, thoughts, and desires, in addition to our physical beings. He works through us to reach others, and He may accomplish that through words but also through our actions and how we relate to people. I recall the Lord once putting on my heart that it was time for my mouth to be saved. I was born again, but I still said whatever I wanted to say whenever I wanted to say it, and often my words were hurtful or improper. I needed to offer my mouth as a living sacrifice to God.

Each of us should ask whether we are living for ourselves and hoping to convince God to give us what we want, or whether we have surrendered our will entirely to His and given our body and all of our faculties to Him for His use. Do you want what God wants for you more than you want what you want for yourself?

When people are young, they have many desires. They may even fear death because there is so much they want to do. But in many cases, by the time they are middle-aged, they have most of what they wanted to possess and have done much of what they wanted to do. Their desires are changing. By the time they are in their latter years, they realize the pursuits that were important to them at age twenty are not nearly as important as they once thought. They may be disappointed and even confused because they thought those things would bring them happiness, but now they find that even with those things, they still are unhappy and lack peace.

If you are a Christian, by the time you are seventy-five years old, you know what is truly important and what is not. You find yourself thinking, *I'm ready anytime Jesus wants to come and take me home.* You also realize that for as long as you remain on earth, doing God's will is the only thing that makes any sense at all.

Personal Reflection

What areas of your life might you be holding back from God and need to surrender to His will for His purpose and use—perhaps your thoughts, your words, your attitudes, your will, your finances, or some other aspect of your life?

_____

_____

_____

_____

_____

_____

Stand Firm

Philippians 1:27–30

*Whatever happens, conduct yourselves in a manner worthy
of the gospel of Christ. Then, whether I come and see you
or only hear about you in my absence, I will know that you
stand firm in the one Spirit, striving together as one for the
faith of the gospel without being frightened in any way by
those who oppose you. This is a sign to them that they will
be destroyed, but that you will be saved—and that by God.
For it has been granted to you on behalf of Christ not only
to believe in him, but also to suffer for him, since you are
going through the same struggle you saw I had, and now
hear that I still have.*

Paul encourages all believers to stand firm and conduct ourselves in ways that glorify God. We are not to be frightened
of those who oppose us, but instead to stand strong and be
fearless. We are not to be frightened by the threats or rejection of those who are against us. We may and probably will
feel fear, but fear is merely an emotion, and we can manage
our emotions, including fear, rather than allowing them to
manage and control us. The reward of such steadfastness is
that our enemies will be destroyed and God will redeem the
painful circumstances we have endured.

Fear is the devil's first choice of weapons to use against us. To fear something is to want to run from it, and that is exactly what the enemy wants. He wants us to run from God's will, to run from difficulty, and to give up on the good things God has asked us to do.

Sometimes God doesn't deliver us from our circumstances as quickly as we know He could, and He uses those times to test and strengthen our ability to endure, be patient, be steadfast, and remain in faith, believing that He is working and trusting that His timing will be perfect. Giving up is not an option for believers in Jesus Christ. God will never give up on us, and we should never give up on Him.

Paul ends this portion of his letter with a statement that is often difficult for people to grasp. He says that it has been granted to us to suffer for Christ. His choice of words suggests that suffering is a privilege, and that is exactly what Paul is trying to say. We have the privilege not only of believing but also of standing firm and suffering as Jesus did, and as Paul did, and as all fully surrendered Christians will at times in their lives. We may experience sickness, being hurt emotionally by someone we love, loss of some kind, or disappointment. We may endure rejection, abandonment, or misunderstanding. Rather than thinking about how much we are being hurt and attacked by the enemy, perhaps we should think more about how we can defeat him as we stand firm in faith. Continuing to trust God, no matter what is happening in our circumstances or how long it takes for our deliverance to come, is the position we should take while waiting for God to vindicate us.

In Matthew 16:17–18, Jesus declares that His church will be built upon the rock of faith and that the gates of hell will not prevail against it. Ephesians 6:16 teaches us that as we lift up the shield of faith, we will quench every fiery dart of the enemy. We are to walk by faith, not by sight (2 Corinthians 5:7) and exhorted to live from faith to faith (Romans 1:17).

Personal Reflection

What are some areas in which the enemy repeatedly tempts you to fear? When he does so, what can you do to stand firm against him?

_____

_____

_____

_____

_____

_____

Like-minded Believers

Philippians 2:1–2

Therefore if you have any encouragement from being united with Christ, if any comfort from his love, if any common sharing in the Spirit, if any tenderness and compassion, then make my joy complete by being like-minded, having the same love, being one in spirit and of one mind.

Paul begins Philippians 2 with an encouragement to be united with Christ. Another way of saying this is that he wants the Philippians to have unity with Christ, to be in agreement with Him. He goes on to say that his joy cannot be complete unless they are like-minded not only with Jesus but also with one another. Like-mindedness does not mean people must think the same way or share the same opinions in all things, but it does mean having a common loyalty to Christ, His truth, and His ways. Such Christ-like unity would certainly require a surrendered will.

I can imagine that God is grieved when there is disunity and strife among believers. I have four children, and it certainly affects my joy if any of them is not getting along with another. God taught me during my early years of ministry how dangerous strife and anger are, and how powerful and wonderful peace and unity are. Our family may disagree on something occasionally, but nobody stays upset for very long—not because we always see eye-to-eye but because we have committed to honoring our unity above our own desires. God never tells us not to get angry, but His Word does say that we are not to let the sun go down on our anger so that we will not give the devil a foothold in our lives (Ephesians 4:26–27).

We flourish in every way when we dwell in peace with God, peace with ourselves, and peace with others (1 Peter 3:11 AMPC). Psalm 133 teaches us that blessing and anointing flow where there is unity. Unity doesn't automatically happen among believers, because people are very different; we have varying perspectives and opinions. Being willing to work to keep peace requires true spiritual maturity, and only Christ-like love will enable us to be peacemakers.

Personal Reflection

How can you work toward greater unity and peace with the people in your life?

_____

_____

_____

_____

_____

Selfish Ambition

Philippians 2:3–4

Do nothing out of selfish ambition or vain conceit. Rather, in humility value others above yourselves, not looking to your own interests but each of you to the interests of the others.

Remember, in this chapter of Philippians, Paul deals with disunity within the church. In Philippians 1, we learned that false teachers had come among them and were causing discord. In chapter 4, we will be introduced to two women who were having a disagreement, and it was severe enough that Paul had to intervene. If strife is not confronted and dealt with, it spreads, causing more and more people to become involved in discord. Paul understood this. This situation was not unique to the Philippians. Paul writes about it also in his letter to the Galatians: "If you bite and devour each other, watch out or you will be destroyed by each other" (Galatians 5:15).

In Philippians 2:3–4, Paul gives us insight into why living in unity and peace is often difficult for people. He speaks of "selfish ambition." Some people work with us or befriend us to advance themselves more than to further the work of

God. The desire for personal prestige is often stronger than the desire for money. People are desperate to feel important, but the truth is that each of us is infinitely important already because God loves and values us.

Working with the Holy Spirit to have pure, unselfish motives requires a willingness to look honestly at our reasons for doing what we do. If our motives are in any way rooted in vain conceit or selfish ambition, we should repent and ask God to help us to be motivated by love and nothing else—love for Jesus and for others. We cannot walk simultaneously in unity with Jesus and in disunity with others. Unselfish love for others requires much more than feelings to support it; it requires a surrendered will.

Far from being filled with selfish ambition, many of the great leaders of the church have lived in such humility that it was often difficult to convince them that God wanted them to step into a high office that would place them in an important and powerful position. William Barclay tells this story in *The New Daily Study Bible on Philippians*:

Ambrose was one of the great figures of the early Church. A great scholar, he was the Roman governor of the province of Liguria and Aemilia in the fourth century, and he had such tender love and concern for the people that they regarded him as a father. The bishop of the district died, and the question of his successor arose. In the middle of the discussion, suddenly a little child's voice was heard: "Ambrose—bishop! Ambrose—bishop!" The whole crowd took up the cry. To Ambrose it was unthinkable. At night he fled to avoid the high office the church was offering him, and it was only the direct intervention and command of the emperor which made him agree to become Bishop of Milan.

Ambrose's story offers us a remarkable example of humility and demonstrates exactly what the apostle Peter was trying to teach when he wrote that we are to humble ourselves under the mighty hand of God and in due time He will exalt us (1 Peter 5:6).

The keynote and final word in this section of Philippians is *others*. Jesus came for others. He lived for others, and He died for others. The more we think about others and how God might want to use us to bless them, the less we have time to be self-focused. The Bible includes more than sixty verses instructing us regarding how to treat others. We are to encourage, be kind and compassionate, forgive, show mercy, become useful and helpful to one another, and learn to love others as Christ loves us (John 13:34). He says that by loving others this way, the world will know that we are His disciples (John 13:35).

Personal Reflection

What can you do to love and serve others today?

_____

_____

_____

_____

_____

_____

_____

CHAPTER 5

THE PATH TO A POWERFUL LIFE

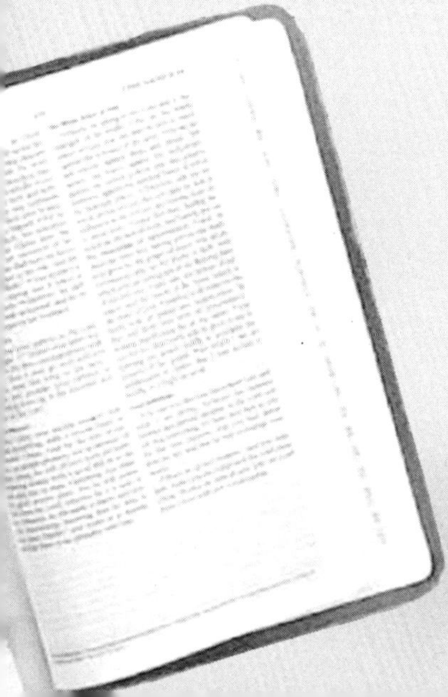

Jesus' Humility and Obedience

Philippians 2:5–8

In your relationships with one another, have the same mindset as Christ Jesus: Who, being in very nature God, did not consider equality with God something to be used to his own advantage; rather, he made himself nothing by taking the very nature of a servant, being made in human likeness. And being found in appearance as a man, he humbled himself by becoming obedient to death—even death on a cross!

Note that Jesus "humbled himself by becoming obedient" to death on a cross. When I think of the word *obedience*, it doesn't bring to mind any thought of convenience or comfort. God is not in the habit of asking us to do things for Him when it is convenient or comfortable or when it fits into our plans. We might even say that God often interrupts us with opportunities to serve Him, and those opportunities often involve serving others. Perhaps I am busy with my plan for the day when a neighbor or friend calls asking if I can take her to a dental appointment because her car won't start. Should I make an excuse and tell her that I would except that I am already otherwise engaged, or should I let love lead me?

We have heard about studying the steps of Jesus, but it might be more helpful to us if we studied the "stops" of Jesus.

In almost every story of Jesus' helping someone, He was on His way somewhere else when He was interrupted by the need of another. But He always stopped. Mark 5:21–43 tells the story of Jairus, one of the synagogue leaders, who asked Jesus to come and heal his daughter, who was apparently almost at the point of death. Jesus went with him but was stopped by someone who also needed His healing touch—a woman who had been bleeding for twelve years. He didn't push her aside or tell her He was busy right then; He stopped and ministered to her. While He was speaking with the woman, a servant from Jairus's house came and told him that his daughter had died. Jesus told him not to be afraid, but to continue believing. Jesus went to Jairus's home and told the girl to get up, and she did, astonishing everyone there.

If we can let go of our plans anytime Jesus calls, we will still accomplish everything we need to do, but we will do it with the joy of knowing we have been obedient. Obedience is the path to a powerful life, but it must be full and complete obedience, not partial obedience.

In the Old Testament, King Saul lost his throne due to par-tial obedience (1 Samuel 15). He did most of what God told him to do, but not all of it. He thought his idea was better than God's, so when he was told to destroy everything he had taken from the enemy, including all the people and their animals and possessions, he destroyed all of it *except* the enemy king and the best of the cattle and lambs. His excuse was that he intended to sacrifice them to the Lord. Whether or not this was Saul's true motive, he still disobeyed God and lost his opportunity to continue to be king. God rejected him as king because he was rebellious and disobedient to Him.

You may think the punishment King Saul received was quite severe, but this wasn't the first time Saul had disobeyed, and it wouldn't be the last. Earlier, through the prophet Samuel, God had told Saul to wait until Samuel returned before offering the evening sacrifice. Saul waited for a long time, but Samuel had not returned, and the people were becoming unhappy and restless. Because Saul thought the people were displeased, he offered the sacrifice thoroughly, even though God had instructed him not to do so (1 Samuel 13:7–14).

Throughout Scripture, we can easily see that people who obeyed God were blessed and enjoyed life with God, while those who disobeyed were not blessed and lived weak, powerless lives.

Personal Reflection

In what areas of your life have you been obedient to God when obedience was difficult for you?

_____

_____

_____

_____

_____

The Doctrine of Kenosis

In Christian theology, the Greek word *kenosis* is used to describe what Philippians 2:5–8 recounts. The fact that Christ "made himself nothing" (v. 7) means that He totally emptied Himself. He made Himself of no reputation. He made Himself completely available to God's will, no matter what that meant for Him.

To understand this more deeply, we must consider that Jesus was and is equal to God the Father, with all the privileges of divine authority. He has existed from all eternity in the form of God. He has full rights as the eternal Son. Yet He willingly laid aside all of this and made Himself a lowly servant in order to do His Father's will. He divested Himself of His divine rights and privileges and unified humanity with divinity (God).

Jesus did not lay aside His divinity, as some people teach. He never ceased to be God, but He did lay aside His rights and privileges and took on human flesh. He became as a man, feeling sorrow, pain, and the weight of our sin, and He did it all for us in obedience to His Father.

Prior to His crucifixion, Jesus was taken captive in the Garden of Gethsemane because Judas, one of His twelve disciples, betrayed Him and sold information about His location to the authorities for thirty pieces of silver (Matthew 26:15). When the men approached Jesus to arrest Him, Peter took out his sword and cut off the ear of one of the high priest's servants. Jesus immediately reached out and healed his ear, asking Peter, "Do you think I cannot call on my Father, and he will at once put at my disposal more than twelve legions of angels? But how then would the Scriptures be fulfilled that say it must happen in this way?" (Matthew 26:53–54).

Jesus could have avoided the pain and shame of everything He went through when He died for us, but He knew what God wanted of Him. Since He was fully surrendered and obedient, He was willing to do it even though He knew it meant pain and sacrifice for Him. Jesus was meek, and to be meek does not mean to be weak. Meekness is actually strength under control. Think of how much strength and self-control it takes to allow oneself to suffer for others when a person—in this case, Jesus—is quite capable of eliminating the suffering and avoiding it altogether.

No Reputation

Although Jesus' fame spread everywhere, He made Himself nothing, according to Philippians 2:7. The New King James Version of the Bible says He "made Himself of no reputation." This tells us He did not have any concern about what people thought of Him, for He had emptied Himself of "self."

Jesus gave up all His rights when He emptied Himself, yet today it seems that people are insisting on their rights with great fervor. As a matter of fact, what some are demanding are not even genuine rights, but rights to which they feel entitled. They have done nothing to earn or deserve what they want, but instead they declare that they have certain rights because they want those rights given to them.

We have many serious problems in our world today

because we are losing the tested, time-honored, godly character traits that people once held dear—qualities such as being
honorable, having integrity, working hard, and keeping our
word. Although our broader culture may have allowed these
things to slip away, those who are diligent to be the kind of
people God wants them to be and to demonstrate godly characteristics from a heart of love for Him will be blessed, no
matter what is happening around them.

Personal Reflection

What godly character traits need to grow and become
stronger in your life?

_____

_____

_____

_____

_____

_____

While I was working on this book, I invited a psychologist
to be a guest on my television program to talk about the ram-
pant increase in teenage suicide over the past few years. She
said that many people are depressed today by relatively small

problems, and that some even commit suicide because they have not been conditioned to endure anything difficult in life. This, of course, is not the only reason people take their own lives. Sometimes the reasons are extremely complicated, and every loss of life is tragic. My guest cited the inability to deal with life's difficulties as one of the biggest problems with many of our youth today.

Contrast this with Jesus, who laid aside His rights and allowed Himself to be mocked, spit upon, beaten, rejected, falsely accused, and crucified. Yet He humbled Himself even to the point of death, and then came His reward.

Many early Christians are known for having given their lives rather than deny Christ. We also see that in parts of the world today. We need more of that kind of commitment.

Without struggle, society becomes weak and unable to endure even minimal hardship without complaining and becoming depressed and discouraged. But God promises a reward to those who persevere. James 1:12 says, "Blessed is the one who perseveres under trial because, having stood the test, that person will receive the crown of life that the Lord has promised to those who love him."

Let us strive to be like Jesus. Let Him be our example in humility and obedience, even if we should suffer in the process.

Reward

Philippians 2:9

Therefore God exalted him to the highest place and gave him the name that is above every name.

Because Jesus completely obeyed His Father, He was exalted to the highest place and given the name that is above every other name. It is a name filled with power, one through which people receive salvation and healing, and one at which every knee "in heaven and on earth and under the earth" must bow (Philippians 2:10). The name of Jesus!

Jesus laid aside His power for a short period of time but was then exalted as a reward. I have said many times that Sunday always comes after Friday. On Friday, He was crucified, but on Sunday He was raised from the dead and exalted on high. In God's Kingdom, resurrection always follows crucifixion. In other words, if we are willing to suffer to do what God asks us to do, He will always reward us at just the right time. God is faithful, and He never forgets our labor for Him.

These four scriptures increase my faith as I wait for God's promised reward, and I hope they will increase yours, too.

And without faith it is impossible to please God, because anyone who comes to him must believe that he exists and that he rewards those who earnestly seek him.

Hebrews 11:6

Humble yourselves, therefore, under God's mighty hand, that he may lift you up in due time.

1 Peter 5:6

Let us not become weary in doing good, for at the proper time we will reap a harvest if we do not give up.

Galatians 6:9

Whatever you do, work at it with all your heart, as working for the Lord, not for human masters, since you know that you will receive an inheritance from the Lord as a reward.

Colossians 3:23–24

Personal Reflection

How have you experienced a reward from the Lord or grown spiritually after a time of difficulty and suffering in your life?

_____

_____

_____

_____

The Name of Jesus

Philippians 2:10–11

That at the name of Jesus every knee should bow, in heaven and on earth and under the earth, and every tongue acknowledge that Jesus Christ is Lord, to the glory of God the Father.

I want us to think for a moment about how powerful the name of Jesus is in our lives as believers. We have been given the power of attorney to use His wonderful and powerful name. Let me explain. My daughter has a power of attorney to use my name and Dave's for various purposes. This means she can sign our checks, do banking for us, close on property if we buy or sell anything, make medical decisions, and handle other business matters for us. She has that privilege only because we trust her, and she always does what we ask her to do with a good attitude.

Jesus has given us His name. We cannot use it to do whatever we want to do, but only to do His will. Furthermore, we must be fully committed to Him in order for the power in His name to work for us. I often say that I did not get Dave's name while we were dating; it was only after we were married, committed to one another for life, that I received his name and was able to use it as my own.

Personal Reflection

Are you merely "dating" Jesus, just calling on Him in emergencies and talking to Him when you are in trouble and need help, or are you fully committed to Him? Have you laid aside your own will and made yourself available for His will anytime He needs you?

_____

_____

_____

_____

_____

One way we demonstrate our love for Jesus is to obey Him. He says that if we love Him, we will obey Him (John 14:15). He also says, "Blessed rather are those who hear the word of God and obey it" (Luke 11:28). After more than forty years of studying God's Word, I can say without hesitation that obedience is the pathway to a blessed and powerful life.

Obedience may seem difficult when we are asked to do something we don't want to do or something that takes us away from our plans, but the enjoyment of a powerful and fruitful life is worth enduring the difficult times. God is counting on us, and I am asking you to make a firm decision to come up higher in your level of obedience. That is my desire, and I believe it is yours, also. We cannot do it without the help of the Holy Spirit, but He is our Helper, and we can depend on Him at all times (John 14:26). God will never ask us to do something without giving us the strength we need to do it. We can do all things through Christ, who is our strength (Philippians 4:13).

CHAPTER 6

OUR GREAT SALVATION

Working Out What God Has Worked into Us

Philippians 2:12

*Therefore, my dear friends, as you have always obeyed—
not only in my presence, but now much more in my
absence—continue to work out your salvation with fear
and trembling.*

These verses have perplexed many people who thought they
had clearly learned in Scripture that salvation is by grace
alone, apart from works. But here, Paul tells us to work out
our own salvation. The simplest way I know to explain this is
to say that Paul is not speaking of working *for* salvation, but
of working it *out* with the help of the Holy Spirit.

We cannot work out what has not been worked into us!
Everything we need to be fruitful, mature sons and daugh-
ters of God is given to us at the time of our new birth—the
moment when we believe that Jesus paid for our sins, died
on our behalf for the forgiveness of our sins, and gave us the
gift of life eternal. The new birth also includes our decision to
believe that He triumphantly rose from the dead and is now
seated in heavenly places waiting for the right time to return
and bring our complete redemption.

When we are born again, something is put into us. We
are given the nature of God, the fruit of the Holy Spirit, right

standing with God through Christ, and many other wonderful blessings. These gifts are deposited into our spirits but need to be worked out of us, into our souls (our minds, wills, and emotions) and ultimately demonstrated through our physical bodies. These three scriptures support this truth.

Therefore, if anyone is in Christ, the new creation has come: The old has gone, the new is here!

2 Corinthians 5:17

God made him who had no sin to be sin for us, so that in him we might become the righteousness of God.

2 Corinthians 5:21

No one born (begotten) of God [deliberately, knowingly, and habitually] practices sin, for God's nature abides in him [His principle of life, the divine sperm, remains permanently within him]; and he cannot practice sinning because he is born (begotten) of God.

1 John 3:9 AMPC

It is very important for us to believe that God has given us all we need in order to do everything He asks of us. His provision comes as seed, for Christ is "the Seed" of God (Galatians 3:16), and as we work with the Holy Spirit, who waters the seed by teaching us and training us in the Word of God, helping us understand and apply it to our lives, this seed grows into the fullness of what He desires us to become.

Let me be as plain as I know how to be, for if anyone misses this point, they will more than likely struggle throughout their life trying to become what they already are. When we are born again, God the Father, Jesus the Son, and God's Spirit come to dwell inside of our human spirit, which has now become His home. He moves in, we might say, and He has promised to never leave us or forsake us (Hebrews 13:5). He is with us always! We are spiritual beings, who have a spirit, a soul, and a body. We need our bodies in order to dwell in this earth, and what we do in the body is what other people see. God's Word teaches us to glorify, or honor, Him in our bodies (1 Corinthians 6:20).

When bringing godly correction to an individual, I have often heard, "But my heart was right!" The person is saying that he or she wanted to do the right thing, and while that is commendable, it should not become an excuse for not actually following through and *doing* what is right. I am reminded of a former employee who was consistently late for work. When confronted about it, she always said, "My heart is right!" One day I finally said, "I'm glad your heart is right, but the fact is that unless you get to work on time, I am going to have to dismiss you from your job." Having the right heart and the right attitude is very important, but sometimes people have a good attitude on the inside and it never makes its way to the outside—their actions and behavior. Part of spiritual maturity is learning to let what's inside of us come out of us. Having a right heart may be a lot easier than having right behavior.

How does what is in us work its way through our soul and

into our bodies (meaning our everyday lives)? When Paul teaches us to "work out" our salvation with fear and trembling, he is saying that it happens as we work with the Holy Spirit toward ever increasing levels of spiritual maturity. The Amplified Bible, Classic Edition amplifies this concept by saying "work out…your own salvation with reverence and awe and trembling (self-distrust, with serious caution, tenderness of conscience, watchfulness against temptation, timidly shrinking from whatever might offend God and discredit the name of Christ" (Philippians 2:12).

Signs of Salvation

There are signs, or indicators, of salvation. No one can receive Christ and not change for the better. However, some people change more than others do, depending on how willing they are to submit to God and change their ways. Some submit to many temptations rather than resisting them and are not careful to avoid doing things that offend God and discredit the name of Christ. These people do not change as much as those who are eager to surrender to God and follow the leading of the Holy Spirit as He guides them to change in certain ways.

These people remain in the baby stage of Christian behavior, of which Paul speaks often. He told the Corinthians that he had to continue giving them the milk of the Word because they were not ready for meat (1 Corinthians 3:2). They had received Christ and were born again, but their lives were not drawing others to Christ, and they have very little or no reward awaiting them in heaven. In verse 3, Paul refers to these Christians as "carnal" (or worldly), which means "related to the flesh," following ordinary impulses and doing what they think and feel rather than what the Holy Spirit is guiding them to do.

Evidence always accompanies true salvation. Signs of salvation include:

- *Effective action.* Christians should be active in serving and obeying God (James 2:17–26).
- *Sincere repentance.* Once we receive Christ, we will be aware of our sin, and it will grieve us and produce in us a desire to change (2 Corinthians 7:10).
- *Loving others.* God is love, and He pours His love into us so we might love Him in return and love others as we love ourselves (Matthew 22:37–39).
- *A consistent display of the fruit of the Holy Spirit:* "Love, joy, peace, forbearance, kindness, goodness, faithfulness, gentleness and self-control" (Galatians 5:22–23). Not only does the display of these qualities make the people around us happy, it makes us happy also. But most importantly, it pleases and glorifies God.

God would never expect us to love had He not given us love as a gift (Romans 5:5). Neither would He expect us to be patient, walk in peace, show kindness, or demonstrate any of the other fruit of the Spirit had He not first worked in us what He now asks us to work out of ourselves.

Personal Reflection

What fruit of salvation have you seen in people who walk closely with God? What evidence of salvation would you like others to see in your life?

_____

_____

_____

_____

_____

_____

Every believer in Christ can truthfully say, "I have all I need to live the life God wants me to live! I can do all things through Christ who is my strength" (Philippians 4:13). As long as we believe we can't do what God asks or think it is too hard, we will never do it, but as we believe God's Word and promises, power is released within us to do what God desires. If we believe right, we will live right.

Jesus says, "By their fruit you will recognize them" (Matthew 7:16). Salvation is a gift from God, given by His grace and received through our faith (Ephesians 2:8). Salvation does not come as the result of our good works, but people will know us by them. Simply hearing the Word of God is not sufficient for a believer. James writes that if we hear and don't do what we heard, we deceive ourselves (James 1:22). We have all known people who attend every church service and can recite Scripture verse after verse, yet when it comes to displaying good fruit, they produce nothing. Such people feel very spiritual, yet they are self-deceived. I have had to deal with what I can truly say were "mean-spirited Christians." That should not be—not ever!

We may be surprised when we get to heaven to discover who is and isn't there.

CHAPTER 7

LET GOD WORK IN YOU AND THROUGH YOU TO BLESS OTHERS

God Works in You

Philippians 2:13

For it is God who works in you to will and to act in order to fulfill his good purpose.

Paul writes that it is God working in us "to will and to act in order to fulfill his good purpose." Some translations render this "to will and to work for His good pleasure" (ESV, AMP, AMPC). In other words, God gives us the desire (will) to work for His pleasure and purpose. It's not something we do for ourselves. We can be assured that since God has given us not only the desire to do good things but also the strength to do them, consistently working with Him will produce the desired result. God's gift of free will is not only freedom to make our own choices, but it is also a great responsibility. God is always leading us to do the right thing, but we don't always submit our will to His. We can choose to do or not to do it, and we may at times feel that two wills are working in us at the same time. We want to do the things God asks of us, but on the other hand we don't want to do them. This is the flesh opposing the desires of the Spirit and the Spirit opposing the desires of the flesh; Paul indicates that the two are continually in conflict with one another (Galatians 5:17).

In the contest between the flesh and the Spirit, if the flesh is stronger, it will win, but if the Spirit is stronger it will win. Just as we feed our physical bodies regularly to keep them strong, we must feed our spirits. We do so by hearing and studying God's Word and by spending time with Him in prayer and fellowship. Be sure to feed your spirit, and it will help you endure the difficulties of life (Proverbs 18:14).

If we do not understand this principle of flesh and Spirit being in conflict with one another, we will be confused. When we are confused, we often make wrong choices. A good truth to remember, which I heard many years ago is, "God is always good, and the devil is always bad." If we follow that one principle when we make our choices, we can avoid many mistakes. I urge you to remember that Satan wants to prevent us from making any kind of progress in life, and he works through our flesh to do it.

When the thought of doing something good for another person comes into your mind, you can be assured the enemy did not put it in you. God did it, and since God has put the thought in you, the enemy will try to fill your mind with opposing thoughts, hoping you will follow your flesh instead of following God's Spirit leading your spirit.

Paul has labored unto weariness teaching the Philippians all they need to know in order to partake of the good life God has provided for them, and he wants to have the joy of knowing his work has not been in vain.

How to Respond When the Way Seems Difficult
Philippians 2:14–18

Do everything without grumbling or arguing, so that you may become blameless and pure, "children of God without fault in a warped and crooked generation." Then you will shine among them like stars in the sky as you hold firmly to the word of life. And then I will be able to boast on the day of Christ that I did not run or labor in vain. But even if I am being poured out like a drink offering on the sacrifice and service coming from your faith, I am glad and rejoice with all of you. So you too should be glad and rejoice with me.

Paul instructs us to do all things without complaining or arguing. The Amplified Bible, Classic Edition states that we are to "do all things without grumbling and faultfinding and complaining."

When we experience trials and tribulation, we should not complain about how hard it is to do what God desires us to do. Actually, times of difficulty are the best times to give praise to and worship God, and they are the best times to be at peace and filled with joy. If we behave in a godly manner only when our circumstances are easy and suitable, then we are no different than an unbeliever.

Paul compares us to "stars in the sky," meaning we are bright lights shining in a dark world as we hold tight to God's Word. Paul knew that if the Philippians did this, he could be assured that he did not run his race for nothing or labor in vain.

It's important for us to think of the example we set for others who are watching us. If they know that we are Christians (followers of Christ), and we murmur and complain like everyone else, we weaken our witness to them, and our lights are not shining. Most of the things God asks of us are simple and help us live ordinary, everyday life in a way that glorifies Him.

Can you get through one day without complaining about anything? Can I? I admit that I have not arrived at the place of perfection, but I have made progress over the years, and I will keep pressing toward God's will.

Personal Reflection

How can you set a good example for people who are watching you, knowing you are a Christian?

_____

_____

_____

_____

_____

_____

No one wants to think that their work has not produced good fruit. As we labor, we should be able to enjoy the fruit of our efforts, and being able to do that strengthens and encourages us to keep pressing forward. We all need encouragement, and we can and should form the habit of encouraging people everywhere we go. Nobody enjoys being in the company of someone who finds fault with them and makes them feel bad about themselves, but we all love people who encourage us. It is commonly said that people may not remember what you said to them when you were with them, but they will always remember how you made them feel.

If you have been wondering what God is calling you to do, you can begin with being an encouraging person who lifts others up and, through your encouragement, energizes them to keep going when their way is hard or they have become weary.

I believe that as we encourage others, we feel encouraged ourselves. I also believe that we reap what we sow, so when we sow encouragement into the lives of other people, God will bring a harvest of encouragement to us. Try giving away some of what you want, and you will be amazed at the harvest you receive (Galatians 6:7).

Jesus Himself says, "Blessed are the merciful, for they will be shown mercy" (Matthew 5:7).

Personal Reflection

In what specific ways can you encourage people
around you today?

_____

_____

_____

_____

_____

_____

Let me encourage you not to fall into the trap of praying for
others to do things for you without taking action to do good
things for them. I call it a trap because it keeps you busy,
but it never helps you. The enemy loves for us to be busy
with things that don't bring the benefit we desire. Worry, for
example, can keep us busy all day long, but all we have at the
end of the day is probably a headache, frustration, anxiety,
and no answers to the problems we are worried about.

Learn to recognize the works of the enemy and resist him.
Submit yourself to God, and "resist the devil, and he will flee
from you" (James 4:7).

Timothy and Epaphroditus, Faithful Servants
Philippians 2:19–30

I hope in the Lord Jesus to send Timothy to you soon, that I also may be cheered when I receive news about you. I have no one else like him, who will show genuine concern for your welfare. For everyone looks out for their own interests, not those of Jesus Christ. But you know that Timothy has proved himself, because as a son with his father he has served with me in the work of the gospel. I hope, therefore, to send him as soon as I see how things go with me. And I am confident in the Lord that I myself will come soon. But I think it is necessary to send back to you Epaphroditus, my brother, co-worker and fellow soldier, who is also your messenger, whom you sent to take care of my needs. For he longs for all of you and is distressed because you heard he was ill. Indeed he was ill, and almost died. But God had mercy on him, and not on him only but also on me, to spare me sorrow upon sorrow. Therefore I am all the more eager to send him, so that when you see him again you may be glad and I may have less anxiety. So then, welcome him in the Lord with great joy, and honor people like him, because he almost died for the work of Christ. He risked his life to make up for the help you yourselves could not give me.

As Paul closes this section of his letter to the Philippians, he tells them that he hopes to send Timothy to them and then he aggressively validates Timothy's ministry to himself and to them. Paul emphasizes that most people look out for their own interests, but Timothy is different. Timothy looks out for the interests of the gospel, and to Paul, he has behaved as a son does to a father.

Although Paul cannot yet send Timothy to Philippi, he does send Epaphroditus—a man the Philippians had sent to him to help him—back to them. Because Paul wanted to be sure the Philippians did not think that Epaphroditus had not fulfilled his duty, he told them he was sending him home because he had worked so hard in the ministry that he became so ill he almost died.

I want you to notice that although God had healed Epaphroditus, Paul still sent him home to rest. He didn't want anyone in Philippi to assume that he was sending Epaphroditus home because he didn't do a good job, so Paul sent him with a testimonial regarding how hard he had worked and how faithful he was. Paul was being courteous and thinking of others, which displayed his love for them.

Epaphroditus needed physical rest, as all people do. In addition, our souls need rest, just as our bodies do. Always remember the importance of living a balanced life in which you work but also rest. When life is out of balance or things are done in excess, it always creates an open door for the enemy. We cannot live a life that blesses others when we do not also take responsibility for our own spiritual, physical, and emotional well-being.

CHAPTER 8

JOY AND TRUST

Abiding Joy

Philippians 3:1

*Further, my brothers and sisters, rejoice in the Lord! It is
no trouble for me to write the same things to you again,
and it is a safeguard for you.*

As I stated in the introduction to this book, Philippians is considered the epistle of joy. In this part of the letter, Paul reminds his readers to rejoice in the Lord. He does not tell us that we can rejoice in *our circumstances* at all times, but that we can rejoice in *the Lord* at all times. Paul rejoiced at all times, and he wanted those he ministered to everywhere to rejoice also.

What does it mean to rejoice in the Lord? It requires thinking about what we have in Christ rather than focusing on our circumstances in life. We are forgiven of all of our sins, our names are written in the Lamb's book of life, and we will live in God's presence eternally. No matter what we do not have, we always have hope, and hope is powerful. We have God's unconditional love, His strength, His peace, His grace, and a host of other wonderful blessings that would make a list too long to put in this book. These are all reasons to rejoice. In addition, God's Word contains more than five thousand promises, and surely that is cause for rejoicing.

I urge you to think more about what you have than what

you don't have. That's the key to abiding joy. To abide means "to live, dwell, and remain with." Joy that abides isn't something that comes and goes. It is indestructible!

Our thinking is the foundation for all of our emotions, and if we desire to have pleasant feelings such as joy and peace, we need to think about things that produce them. Here is one great promise of God that causes me to rejoice: "And we know that in all things God works for the good of those who love him, who have been called according to his purpose" (Romans 8:28).

H. A. Ironside writes in his *Notes on the Epistle to the Philippians,* "It is not only the Christian's privilege, but also his duty to rejoice constantly in the Lord."

Personal Reflection

Stop and think about some of the blessings in your life. Why are they reasons to rejoice?

_____

_____

_____

_____

_____

_____

The Philippian believers to whom Paul writes faced a great possibility of the same types of persecution—and even death—that threatened him. Although they might endure hardship, because of their faith, nothing could separate them from the love of God found in Christ Jesus (Romans 8:35–39). The great preacher John Wesley managed to abide in joy, though he faced cruel hardship. There is a story about John Wesley and John Nelson, who together carried out a mission in Cornwall. The two of them slept on the floor, one of them using a coat for a pillow and the other using a book filled with notes on the New Testament. Wesley reportedly woke up one night, and finding Nelson also awake, poked him in the side and said, "Brother Nelson, let us be of good cheer: I have one whole side yet, for the skin is off on but one side." Wesley had a habit of accepting life's discomforts with humor, and we should do the same thing.

My speaking schedule has required me to travel a great deal over the years, and Dave and I have experienced many inconvenient and irritating circumstances during that time. For example, recently, twice in one month the water went off on the floor of the hotel where our room was located. What are the chances that such an unusual occurrence would happen two times in one month in two different hotels? Not likely, so we decided the enemy was merely trying to irritate us, and we refused to be irritated. I laughed and said, "If the water doesn't come back on by 7:00 a.m., I will have to find another room in the hotel where I can get ready for the day, because I cannot go to a conference looking the way I do, without the opportunity to clean up and fix my hair." I prayed, asking God to somehow solve the problem with the water by 7:00 a.m., and at 6:55 a.m., an engineer knocked on the door to tell us the water was back on.

Perhaps if we prayed and kept our joy instead of becoming upset and losing it, we would see more amazing answers to prayer. Just as we can go to the sink and turn on the water, we can turn on our joy by deciding to have godly perspectives on our circumstances. I can assure you that God doesn't worry or fret over the conditions in the world, and we don't have to, either. We should be actively doing whatever God might lead us to do, but He never leads us to worry or fret. As a matter of fact, God's Word tells us not to fret over evildoers, because they will soon wither like the grass (Psalm 37:1–2).

Personal Reflection

In what situations can you choose to be joyful today?

_____

_____

_____

_____

_____

_____

The Necessity of Repetition

Paul had apparently written to the Philippians at other times, sending them the same message he communicates in this epistle. But he states in Philippians 3:1 that writing the same things to them again is no trouble for him, and that, in fact, it is a safeguard to them.

How many of us can hear something one time, put it into action, and never forget it? Not many, I would think. God graciously reminds us of things that we have ceased to focus on. His reminders may come through hearing a preacher's message, reading a book, or by the Holy Spirit's bringing them to our remembrance. A friend could mention something we need to hear, or we could come across it in our daily Bible study.

Sometimes when we are preparing to hear a sermon and the speaker announces a topic we've already heard about many times, we think we don't need to hear it talked about again. I would encourage us all not to think this way, because we all need repetition and reminders in order to stay on the right and narrow path in life. As human beings, we crave novelty and new and exciting things, but the gospel is not intended to entertain us; it is designed to instruct us in godly living. We can be assured that when we need something new, God will meet that need along with reminding us of the important things we have learned and do not need to forget.

As a Bible teacher for close to forty-five years, I often crave new material to teach and new sermons to preach, and I have been concerned that people might get tired of hearing things they have heard in the past. However, numerous people have reassured me that each time they hear the truth preached—even if they have heard something similar previously—they need it and benefit from it. Often, they see or realize truths they did not realize previously. Let us be thankful that the truth of God's Word—no matter how many times we hear it—is always fresh and full of life. Each time we hear the Word or meditate on it, it becomes more deeply rooted in us, and the enemy of our souls has more difficulty taking it from us through his lies and deceptions.

Remain Watchful

Philippians 3:2–4

Watch out for those dogs, those evildoers, those mutilators
of the flesh. For it is we who are the circumcision, we who
serve God by his Spirit, who boast in Christ Jesus, and
who put no confidence in the flesh—though I myself have
reasons for such confidence.

Paul's tone changes now to one of warning. It occurred regularly that when Paul preached, Jews followed him and told
the Christians to whom he ministered that they needed to
be circumcised in order to please God. They worked hard
to undo what Paul was doing. Paul taught that salvation
comes by grace alone and not by our own works (Ephesians
2:8–9). Salvation is a gift and can never be earned. Paul
preached that this offer was for all people from all nations.
The Jews, however, taught that one could only be saved by
doing countless deeds in observance of the law and that circumcision was the most important of all the laws for them to
obey.

Paul was apparently weary of the Jews' attempts to negate
his work with their inaccurate doctrine, so he called them
"dogs." He said, basically, "Beware of the dogs." Today, we

think of dogs as our pets; we keep them in our homes and they are well loved. But during Jesus' day, dogs were strays that roamed the streets and ate garbage. They sometimes ran in packs and could be dangerous. Dogs in those days were considered to be the lowest of low life forms, despicable and dangerous.

The Jews called the Gentiles "dogs" because of their hatred for them, and now Paul calls these Jews who were trying to pervert the gospel and bring people back under the law "dogs." He also calls them "evildoers" and "mutilators of the flesh."

In Philippians 3:3, Paul refers to believers as those "who are the circumcision." Circumcision for the Jew was nothing more than a cutting away of part of the flesh. When Abraham first received God's instruction to circumcise all males, it was a sign of a covenant with God. The circumcised person was saying through the circumcision that he belonged to God and was choosing to serve Him with his life (Genesis 17:10–14). But to the Jews of Paul's day, circumcision was only a physical mark. It had lost its significance as a sign of covenant relationship with God and did not represent a commitment to God, but was merely a law that many still followed.

For people who were circumcised under the Old Covenant to have a right relationship with God, their hearts had to also be circumcised, and they were instructed not to be stubborn (Deuteronomy 10:16). Jeremiah told the people they needed a circumcised ear that would hear and follow God (Jeremiah 6:10 AMPC), and Moses, the writer of Exodus, mentions his uncircumcised lips as being a problem (Exodus 6:12 NKJV).

For the New Testament Christian, the mark of circumcision in the flesh is no longer required, because God the Father has already done the work needed to bring us into right relationship with Him by sacrificing His Son Jesus as payment for our sins. What good news! Our sins have been forgiven! Circumcision of male babies is often performed today by the medical community because some think it is healthier than not circumcising, not because it makes one right with God.

Paul used the opportunity of writing to the Philippians to try to send the Jews the message that if their circumcision was only a mutilation of the flesh, it was of no value, and to let them know that they needed an inner circumcision, a circumcision of the heart.

It is totally possible for people to go through religious exercises and yet have hearts that are far away from God. People may attend church regularly and yet have hearts filled with bitterness and hatred. God looks at our hearts rather than our outward appearance (1 Samuel 16:7), and if our hearts are not right, then nothing we do to supposedly worship Him has any real meaning.

The Jews trusted themselves and were very proud of all their good works, but the true Christian trusts God alone.

Christians know that none of our good works can save us or put God in our debt.

No Confidence in the Flesh

Paul declares to the Christians that they are the true circumcision, and they "serve God by his Spirit," and they rejoice in Jesus and "put no confidence in the flesh." In order to say, as Paul says in Philippians 3:3, that we put no confidence in the flesh, we should understand more fully what that means.

Putting no confidence in the flesh means that we don't trust ourselves or other people for salvation. In every aspect of our lives, our hope and confidence are in Christ. We have all disappointed ourselves and done things we never thought we would do, and others have disappointed us and let us down when we needed them most. So, we have learned by experience that only God can be wholly counted on to never disappoint us or to never leave or forsake us. He is faithful, and will always fulfill His promises. If we put our confidence (trust) in anything or anyone other than Jesus, we will be living on shaky ground. But those who trust in God will have a firm and solid foundation on which to live. Let each of us ask ourselves where we place our confidence, making sure it is not misplaced, but that it is in Christ and Christ alone.

Personal Reflection

Where do you place your trust? Is it in Christ alone?

_____

_____

_____

_____

_____

_____

_____

CHAPTER 9

—◁◦▷—

TRUE CONFIDENCE
AND TRUE VALUE

The Right Kind of Confidence

Philippians 3:4–7

*If someone else thinks they have reasons to put confidence
in the flesh, I have more: circumcised on the eighth day,
of the people of Israel, of the tribe of Benjamin, a Hebrew
of Hebrews; in regard to the law, a Pharisee; as for zeal,
persecuting the church; as for righteousness based on
the law, faultless. But whatever were gains to me I now
consider loss for the sake of Christ.*

It is quite easy to put no confidence in ourselves if we feel
we have nothing about which to be confident. But if we feel
we have many natural reasons for self-confidence, it is even
more difficult to learn that putting our confidence in anyone
other than Christ is foolish and a waste of time. It actually
slows down our success rather than helping it.

As I mentioned in the previous chapter, God wants us to
be totally dependent upon Him, not to be independent. In
John 15, Jesus teaches that we are the branches and He is the
Vine, and He urges us to abide (live, dwell, remain) in Him.
He says that those who abide in Him will bear much fruit
(John 15:5).

While teaching the Bible, I have often used an example
that I believe helps make this point clearly. I get a branch that

has been broken off of a vine. On the first day of a conference, we look at it and see that it has plenty of plump, life-filled leaves. By the third day of the conference, the leaves are crispy around the edges and we can easily see that they are dying. This is a picture of what happens to us when we try to be independent of God and be dependent on ourselves or others. When we are not connected to Him, we will experience a loss of fulfillment and success. Like the leaves in the example, we will see signs of drying up and a diminishing of our quality of life.

Personal Reflection

Have you ever felt spiritually dry? If you have drifted away from Christ, how can you reconnect with Him?

_____

_____

_____

_____

_____

_____

We encourage our children to grow up and be independent, but our relationship with God is different than the ones we have with our children. Of course, He wants us to mature spiritually and take responsibility for ourselves but always with His will in mind, admitting that we need His help in order to succeed. Jesus says we must come to Him as a little child would come (Matthew 18:2–3). Self-reliance is rooted in a need to feel proud of what we have accomplished, but we must avoid that pride and the temptation to take the glory (meaning the credit due) of our accomplishments for ourselves.

We have heard people say, "I'm a self-made person." This means they think they have the life they have because they have worked hard and done it without relying on anyone else. The world applauds the "self-made" person, but living this way saddens God because it prevents people from receiving from Him the divine help they could have had. No matter how great people may think their lives are without God, life is always much, much better with Him.

A person may achieve success as far as the world is concerned but have no peace or joy, which are the true marks of success. People may have money, but they have used others to get it. They have missed the joy of truly loving people and helping them succeed. Many who appear to be the most successful people in the world are in reality very miserable and unhappy.

Personal Reflection

What is the difference between having true, godly joy and enjoying worldly success?

_____

_____

_____

_____

_____

_____

_____

Jesus says that those who are weary and overburdened can come to Him and He will give them rest for their souls (Matthew 11:28). This invitation is, I believe, directed to all the self-reliant, self-confident people who are worn-out from trying to do things on their own.

Paul had a great deal to be self-confident about. He had been proud of each of his hard-earned accomplishments until the day he met Christ. That day Paul began to see things in his life in a different way. Here is an impressive list of credentials in which he could have chosen to place his confidence, based primarily on Philippians 3:5–6:

- He was born under the Abrahamic covenant.
- He carried the mark of covenant with God (circumcision).
- He was highly educated.
- He was a Pharisee among Pharisees. A chief Pharisee!
- He lived an exemplary, righteous life, following the laws and traditions passed down from previous generations.
- He had the "right" parents who came from the "right" bloodline.
- He was from the tribe of Benjamin. Being a Benjamite was a source of natural pride. The tribes of Benjamin and Judah were the only ones to remain faithful when all others rebelled against David. These two tribes formed the Kingdom of Judah.
- He was a Jew, and he was a Roman citizen. Very few Jews ever attained Roman citizenship (Acts 22:3, 26–27).
- He was a persecutor of the newfound Christians, the followers of Christ, who were very unpopular in certain circles. He hunted them down, tried to force them to blaspheme, and handed them over to be imprisoned. He felt this was the right thing to do and viewed this persecution as zealously serving God. Yet, later in life, he said that he had zeal without knowledge.

Paul's impressive list of qualities and accomplishments gave him many reasons to be confident in the flesh. However, once Paul met Christ and experienced His grace, he realized that nothing he did could be of any value unless Jesus was first in his life at all times and in all things.

I can only imagine that it may have taken Paul a bit of time to let go of all his past accomplishments as reasons to be confident, but he did it. We should also be able to release the things that have given us confidence and find our confidence in Christ alone.

Nothing Has Value apart from Christ

Philippians 3:8–9

What is more, I consider everything a loss because of the surpassing worth of knowing Christ Jesus my Lord, for whose sake I have lost all things. I consider them garbage, that I may gain Christ and be found in him, not having a righteousness of my own that comes from the law, but that which is through faith in Christ—the righteousness that comes from God on the basis of faith.

Once enlightened by Christ, Paul considered all the things he once thought made him righteous before God to be mere trash (garbage) compared to the privilege of knowing Christ Jesus.

The things in which he once placed his hope he now saw as worthless. Imagine all the time and effort Paul had put into being well known and admired, self-important and self-assured. His reputation with people had been more important to him than anything else. His entire worth and value as a man had previously been tied to these attributes and accolades. But once he met Jesus, all of that changed. I think a lot of us can say that once we met Jesus, everything changed.

Personal Reflection

In your life, how has everything changed since you met Jesus?

_____

_____

_____

_____

_____

_____

Paul reached the point where he wanted more than anything else to be found and known as one who was considered to be "in Christ," with no righteousness of his own—that his right standing with God was only in knowing Christ and belonging to Him and in nothing else.

Isaiah tells us that all of our own righteousness is like filthy rags: "All of us have become like one who is unclean, and all our righteous acts are like filthy rags; we all shrivel up like a leaf, and like the wind our sins sweep us away" (Isaiah 64:6).

Paul never lost his first love as so many people do. He passionately pressed on to know Jesus and become like Him in all of his ways from the day he met Jesus until the day he died.

I would encourage you to follow Paul's example and to be sure you stay strong in your faith and guard against letting what was once a raging fire in your heart become a pile of barely glowing embers. This occurs as we begin to seek other things and allow them to become more important to us than Jesus is. We get busy with life and find we have no time to seek God through His Word and prayer on a daily basis. People may have all the things money can buy yet lose all that money can never buy—such as a deep relationship with God through Christ, the joy of helping others, and good relationships with family and friends. I once read that people who are dying never ask for their bank balance; they want God, family, and friends around them. Sadly, if we spend no time building these relationships while we are living and healthy, they won't be available when we want and need them.

We should all take time occasionally to examine our lives and ask ourselves if we are putting our time into lasting pursuits or if we are spending too much time on things that have no true meaning. We can spend our lives climbing the ladder of success only to find when we reach the top that our ladder is leaning against the wrong building. We reap according to what we sow (Galatians 6:7); therefore, if we don't sow time and effort into the right things, we cannot expect to have right results. Be wise and do now what you will be happy and satisfied with later.

Personal Reflection

How can you begin spending more of your time and
energy on things that truly matter?

_____

_____

_____

_____

_____

_____

_____

_____

I love the scriptures in this section and the ones we will
study in the next section because, through them, I can sense
the passion in Paul's desire. He did not have an ordinary
desire, but a passionate desire for the kind of righteousness
that was acceptable to God. Paul dedicated his life to pursuing this passion and to helping others pursue it, too.

Personal Reflection

What is the passionate pursuit of your life right now? Will it satisfy you once you attain it? Where is your righteousness found? Is it in your accomplishments or in Christ alone?

_____

_____

_____

_____

_____

_____

_____

_____

I know the joy Paul felt after realizing the truth that nothing has any value apart from Christ because I have experienced it myself. I will never forget the years I spent struggling to please God through my own good works. I won't forget how important my reputation was to me and how I often compromised on important things simply to have people think well of me.

Living as I have just described eventually becomes a burden too heavy for any of us to bear. Many years of such striving and still always feeling that we have come up short leaves us exhausted. The only thing we know to do is "try harder," but it never works; we only become more exhausted and frustrated.

Upon discovering that we can give up all of our striving and self-effort and have Christ and His righteousness—instead of trying to earn righteousness ourselves—a burden lifts from us, and we can begin to enjoy God and the life He has given us. People often express the amazing joy and peace they have had since receiving that revelation from God.

Paul's unforgettable experience on the road to Damascus (Acts 9) totally ruined him for anything other than serving God with all humility, and I pray that our realization of what God has done for us in and through Christ will have the same effect on our lives.

CHAPTER 10

KNOWING CHRIST AND THE POWER OF HIS RESURRECTION

Avoiding Stagnation

Philippians 3:10–11

I want to know Christ—yes, to know the power of his resurrection and participation in his sufferings, becoming like him in his death, and so, somehow, attaining to the resurrection from the dead.

I am partial to the Amplified Bible, Classic Edition rendering of Philippians 3:10, because it has helped me understand what Paul meant when he said he wanted to know Christ and the power of His resurrection:

> [For my determined purpose is] that I may know Him [that I may progressively become more deeply and intimately acquainted with Him, perceiving and recognizing and understanding the wonders of His Person more strongly and more clearly], and that I may in that same way come to know the power outflowing from His resurrection [which it exerts over believers], and that I may so share His sufferings as to be continually transformed [in spirit into His likeness even] to His death.

Let me ask you to stop and feel the depth of the cry of Paul's heart in this passage. He wasn't satisfied with merely knowing about Jesus or even just knowing Him a little; he wanted to know Him deeply and intimately. That goal, in fact, was his determined purpose. Many people know about Jesus or believe that He exists, but a much richer quality of life with Him is available to us. What fuels intimacy with God is time and including Him in every area of our lives.

Spending time with people and seeing them in all kinds of situations is the only way to truly know them. Our family is very close, and although my children are all adults who have their own families, they still call their mom and tell me what they are doing, or they share their joys or heartaches with Dave and me. You can love all your children the same yet feel closer to the ones who include you in their lives and also do things for you.

I believe the same principle applies to our relationship with God. It seems that the apostle John had a special, very intimate relationship with Jesus. He referred to himself as the disciple whom Jesus loved (John 13:23; 19:26). That might sound a bit haughty on his part, but it wasn't. John simply loved Jesus and had a real revelation of how much Jesus loved him. His goal, like Paul's, was intimacy with Jesus. I think anyone can be as close to God as he or she wants to be. The level of intimacy a person enjoys with Him depends simply on how much time he or she is willing to put into building the relationship.

The time I am talking about is not an hour spent sitting in a church once a week. It is about including God in all we do.

He is never more than one thought away from us, so I encourage you to think of Him often, whisper your gratitude to Him for different things all throughout the day, and ask for His help in everything, even in seemingly insignificant things. I ask the Lord to help me before I try to put in my contact lenses, before I work out, or before I approach any project, no matter how small it might be. I am sorry for the times I have an independent attitude and spend the day doing many things without even asking for His help. You might say, "Well, Joyce, you got the things done anyway, so what difference does it make if you didn't ask for God's help?" I may have gotten the things done, but how much more joyfully, more easily, and perhaps more quickly could I have accomplished them with God's help?

I certainly have not perfected this spiritual discipline. There have been plenty of times when I've gone about my busy schedule and suddenly the day was over, and I realized I hadn't thought of the Lord all day. I'm not suggesting that God will never help us unless we ask for His help in each specific task we undertake, but I believe we honor Him when we do, and doing so is a way to keep Him in our thoughts. I am hoping to establish the importance of always having the realization of how much we need the Holy Spirit's help in all we do. This is not a law we must follow but a privilege we have, so why not take advantage of it?

Personal Reflection

How can you know Jesus deeply and intimately?

_____

_____

_____

_____

_____

_____

_____

_____

Finding Your Path

Because each of us has a different God-given temperament, He gives us the freedom to find our own pathway into intimacy with Him. It is not a formula we follow, but a person we pursue. Since we are unique individuals, each different from one another, we sense God's presence in various ways. One person may feel close to God when in nature, some while listening to music, some in quiet times, some when accomplishing something they believe will glorify Him, and others in Bible study or times of prayer. The pathway we choose is not important as long as we end up with the desired result. The beauty of following the leadership of the Holy Spirit is that He will lead each of us in a way that is right for us. We don't have rules and regulations attached to our personal relationship with Him; we simply need to seek and pursue Him with all of our heart. Jesus is interested in our heart's desire, not our methods.

In my life right now, I have the type of schedule that allows me to get up in the morning and enjoy as much quiet time with God as I would like. But a young mother of four children may not have that privilege, so the Holy Spirit will give her other opportunities that may be better suited for her lifestyle. A working person who can't take the time in the morning can choose to use their lunch break to spend time with God. My husband did that for many years. He ate his lunch and then spent the remainder of his hour-long lunch period walking outside around his work area and praying. He has told me that it was during those times that he became certain in his heart that one day he would quit his job in engineering and be in full-time ministry. One thing is for sure: If we are diligent in seeking God, He will reveal Himself to us and give us direction for our lives.

I want to challenge you to start looking for special times you can spend with the Lord. It may be a short time or a long time, but remember that the time invested will determine your level of intimacy. God promises that if we seek Him with our whole heart, we will find Him (Jeremiah 29:13).

Personal Reflection

Are there ways in which you need to adjust your schedule in order to prioritize your relationship with God? What are they?

_____

_____

_____

_____

_____

_____

_____

Resurrection Life

What is the resurrection life Paul writes about in Philippians 3:11? We know there was a resurrection when Jesus rose from the dead, but I believe Paul may have been thinking about another type of resurrection. On a practical level, I believe the kind of resurrection life Paul has in mind here is found in the knowledge of who God is—a knowledge that allows us to deal with, and yet live above, the storms of life.

We cannot avoid all the difficulties life brings, but we can have a strong faith in God that allows us to endure whatever comes with a joyful heart. An airplane can fly through storms and go to a higher altitude that takes it above the storm, and I believe we can do the same. I think that was the type of resurrection life Paul sought to attain and encouraged others to seek.

Why did Paul pray in Philippians 3:10 to participate in Jesus' sufferings, "becoming like him in his death"? He knew there could be no resurrection without death to ourselves. Anyone who wants to be close to God will need to welcome the process of transformation. When Jesus comes to live in someone's heart, that person's nature is changed. But as we have studied previously, what is in us must be worked out of us, and that is often painful. In order to fully follow God, each of us must be willing to "die" to, or let go of, many things that may seem important to us.

Why is transformation (change) painful? If we think about it in a practical way, it is easy to understand. If the Lord is teaching me humility, He will have to guide me into situations in which my flesh would tend to be prideful. But as I submit to God's will, I learn humility by experience. I will experience the pain of dying to self-will, but at the end of it, my reward will be more peace, joy, and spiritual maturity.

If God is teaching me to be more generous, He may lead me to give away something that I really want to keep. Believe me, it is painful to the flesh to give away what it wants to keep. Another great example is the pain we may experience when we follow God's will and forgive and bless our enemies.

I believe that doing the right thing when it feels wrong means we are growing spiritually. If you are already able to easily and quickly forgive those who hurt you, then you are already mature in that area, but if it is still difficult for you, the good news is that every time you practice it, you grow spiritually. It seems to me that we are always growing in some area, and after a while we have victory through the grace of our Lord Jesus Christ, and then we begin to grow in another area.

I could give you hundreds of examples just from my own experience, but I am sure you have plenty of examples of your own. The good news is that the more we are transformed into His image, the less it hurts when we don't get our way. We don't have to have perfect circumstances in order to have peace and joy. We no longer waste days in self-pity or discouragement. If you desire this kind of victory in your life, then pray as Paul did that you might know Christ and the power of His resurrection, and share in His sufferings in order to be transformed into His image.

The longer you walk with God, the more you will know Him. We know Him and His ways from studying the Bible, but also from our experiences with Him. We can begin studying the Bible as soon as we are born again, but experience takes time. As the years pass, if we remain steadfast in our commitment to Him, we will experience the joy of answered prayer and the faithfulness of God. We will ultimately understand that what we once thought was our worst enemy has now become our best friend, simply because it helped us become who God wants us to be.

Personal Reflection

What experiences have helped you grow spiritually? How have you come to know God deeply through them?

_____

_____

_____

_____

_____

_____

_____

CHAPTER 11

---◇---

PRESSING ON IN FAITH

Learning to Live in the Present Moment
Philippians 3:12–14

Not that I have already obtained all this, or have already arrived at my goal, but I press on to take hold of that for which Christ Jesus took hold of me. Brothers and sisters, I do not consider myself yet to have taken hold of it. But one thing I do: Forgetting what is behind and straining toward what is ahead, I press on toward the goal to win the prize for which God has called me heavenward in Christ Jesus.

Paul wants to make clear to his readers that he does not consider himself to have arrived at the fullness of all of his spiritual goals. He desires to be perfect, but he admits he has not reached that place. While it is often good to share our victories with others, it is also good to share our journeys. Paul was on his way to reaching his goals but readily admitted that he had not attained them. Our victory stories come after our journeys are complete, but to share only our victories without being honest about the challenges, difficulties, and pain of the journey never really helps people who are hurting. In fact, it may confuse them and make them wonder why others always seem to be enjoying victory while they are still in a difficult place with painful circumstances.

If we fear being vulnerable, we will often pretend

everything is wonderful when, in reality, we are struggling and hurting. Paul didn't do that. He shared many victories but did not exclude his weaknesses and struggles from his writing.

If you were asked what the most important day in your life has been, what would you say? Some might say it was the day they married, graduated from college, or had their first child. While all of those are wonderful occasions, none of those answers would be correct, because the most important day of any of our lives is *today*! Many important days hold memories we cherish, but nothing compares to the importance of today, because today matters more than you may realize.

Paul states that his one aspiration (hope, wish, desire) was to let go of those things that were behind and press toward the full will of God. Paul knew he could not make progress today if he held on to yesterday's mistakes. This is a very powerful truth, which is important for us to realize. Today holds possibilities for those who embrace it and look earnestly for what it may hold for them. Today is very important because once it is gone, you can never get it back again. Don't waste it worrying about the mistakes of the past.

I struggled with guilt and condemnation in a major way for close to fifty years. Having been abused sexually by my father and growing up in a home that was a mixture of my father's violence and abuse and my mother's fear and timidity, I did not have many opportunities to feel good about myself. I always assumed that something was wrong with me for my father to want to treat me in the despicable way he did. I had a recording that was on a loop playing over and over in my mind that said, "What's wrong with me? What's wrong with me?"

I have learned that carrying a burden of guilt leaves us weary, worn-out, and spiritually, mentally, emotionally, and physically exhausted. We were not built for guilt! God created us in His own image with a desire for us to love Him, love others, and love ourselves. He also wants us to love and fully enjoy our lives. But we cannot do that if we are stuck in our past mistakes, hurts, and injustices. Scripture instructs us to repent of our sins, to forgive those who hurt and wound us, and to totally let go of things from the past.

The prophet Isaiah, delivering a message from God, says, "Forget the former things; do not dwell on the past. See, I am doing a new thing! Now it springs up; do you not perceive it?" (Isaiah 43:18–19).

I carried a burden of guilt for many years, but even worse than guilt, I had shame—shame that was toxic. It was poison to my soul. I was not merely ashamed of what had been done to me, but at the very core of my being I was ashamed of myself because it had happened. I assumed that somehow it was my fault. Then I saw in Scripture that instead of shame, God would give me a double portion of all that had been stolen from me (Isaiah 61:7). Isaiah also prophesied that we would be delivered from the shame of our youth (Isaiah 54:4). I took these promises as my own, and although the journey was not easy, victory did come in due time.

If we do not let go of the past, we will miss the new things that God is doing in our lives. God is ready to help us any-time we need help, but we cannot hold on to old things and take hold of new things at the same time.

Personal Reflection

Have guilt and shame kept you bound to the past? Will you ask God today to help you accept His for-giveness and to help you move forward? I encourage you to read and reread the Bible verses mentioned in this chapter to help establish in your heart and mind the truth that God wants to set you free to enjoy a wonderful future.

_____

_____

_____

_____

_____

_____

_____

Steps of Faith

Some people hang on to old situations or emotions even though they are painful because they are at least familiar.

They are afraid to see what the future holds. "After all," they ask themselves, "what if I don't like the new thing, or what if I end up with nothing?" God's Kingdom operates differently than the kingdom of this world. God requires us to take steps of faith without knowing exactly what we are stepping into. Only after we have done that will He show us what He can do.

Perhaps you can relate to Robert's situation. Robert had worked at the same company, doing the same job, for sixteen years. He worked hard, but he never received any appreciation for a job well done. He just went to work, did his job, and then went home, only to do the same thing the next day and the next. If he really thought about it, he didn't even like the work he was doing; it was not fulfilling to him, nor did it make use of his best abilities. Nothing about the job challenged or inspired him.

Robert was a Christian, and one day as he was praying and asking God to give him more joy, a God-inspired thought came to him: *Robert, I can't give you joy if you are not going to follow your heart and step out into something new.* Robert knew right away that it was God speaking to him, for it was not the first time he had heard these whispers deep in his heart. But there was a problem: Robert always played it safe. He wasn't very aggressive, and he lived with a lot of fear. He believed what he felt more than he believed God's Word to him. His wife, Julie, greatly encouraged him to at least begin looking for a different job. Immediately his head was filled with reasons he could not do it. First, he wasn't even sure what he wanted to do, and second, why would anyone hire someone in a field in which he had no experience at all?

Sometimes we do not know what we will truly enjoy until we simply try different things. Robert had always worked in accounting, so he decided to go to night school and study to become a CPA. He graduated with top grades and started his own business on the side while still keeping his job to support his family. It was very hard for a while because of all the extra hours he had to work, but his wife pitched in and made sure he didn't have to do anything toward the upkeep of their home during that time. After about three years, Robert finally took the step of faith to quit his job and work full-time at his own business. The work was similar to what he had always done, but now he had much more variety, freedom, and responsibility, which he found to be exhilarating. His business prospered, and eventually he had several other accountants working for him.

Robert would have missed all these blessings had he never taken that first step to do something to change his situation. This example shows us one way of letting go of the past, but there are many ways depending on what "past" you are hanging on to. If it is past sin, any sin you have committed has already been paid for. That happened when Jesus died on the cross. All you need to do is repent of your sin, believe God's Word, and begin behaving as someone who is loved and totally forgiven (1 John 1:9). God not only forgives you, but He also forgets your past (Isaiah 43:25; Hebrews 10:17). I urge you to believe this and receive it as a gift from Him, with gratitude and joy.

You may be thinking what I thought for years: *I have repented, but I still feel guilty.* I finally realized that God's Word is more reliable than my feelings, and once I repented, I could choose to let go of the past and take hold of the new day God wanted me to embrace. My feelings didn't change right away, but my attitude and thoughts did, and eventually my feelings changed as well.

I can sense in Paul's writing while dealing with this subject that it was very important for him personally not only to refuse to continue to feel guilty after he had repented but also to teach others the uselessness of guilt over past events that have been forgiven.

Proverbs 4:25–27 says, "Let your eyes look straight ahead; fix your gaze directly before you. Give careful thought to the paths for your feet and be steadfast in all your ways. Do not turn to the right or the left; keep your foot from evil."

If we were meant to look at the past all the time, we would have eyes in the back of our heads. Our eyes are arranged in such a way that looking straight ahead is the best and most comfortable way to look. If you are someone who suffers from excessive guilt, please look up the Scripture references I have given and meditate on them, realizing you are a new creature in Christ and you don't have to live in the past.

CHAPTER 12

◆—◇—◆

LET GO AND GROW

A Sign of Spiritual Maturity

Philippians 3:15–16

All of us, then, who are mature should take such a view of things. And if on some point you think differently, that too God will make clear to you. Only let us live up to what we have already attained.

While dealing with the subject of guilt and shame, Paul makes an important statement that has helped me tremendously, and I want to make sure you don't miss the power of it. He says, "All of us, then, who are mature should take such a view of things" (Philippians 3:15). He goes on to indicate that if we are missing something we need to see, then God will make it clear to us. In the meantime, live in the truth you have already gained and keep growing.

Why is this so important? Paul is helping us understand that living under guilt once we have repented and received forgiveness is the baby stage of Christianity. Only those who are spiritually mature will believe God's Word more than they believe how they feel or even what they think. Some people think that continually demeaning or berating themselves for their sin is somehow a positive spiritual quality, but that thinking does not agree with Scripture.

I once knew a woman who loved God very much. She had been taught that suffering for her sin was pleasing to God, so she often wore a scratchy patch of wool against her skin under her clothing, and it was very uncomfortable. That way, she reasoned, her misery would remind her of how wretched she was. That theology is not at all consistent with God's Word. Jesus suffered and paid for our sins, and He did a complete and perfect job. He does not need us to add anything to it, not even our burden of guilt.

Is guilt anything other than trying to pay for our sins? I think not! Can we pay by making ourselves miserable and refusing to enjoy life? No! We cannot pay a debt that has already been paid, and to keep trying to pay it, I believe, dishonors Jesus' sacrifice.

Paul writes that he *presses on* (Philippians 3:14). I believe we can assume that the devil tried to hold him in the memory of his past mistakes, just as he does us. Thankfully, when we submit ourselves to God, we can resist the devil and he will flee (James 4:7). Living the victorious Christian life often requires pressing in and pressing on by choosing to move forward beyond guilt, shame, and condemnation. It may require us to face various tests that make us uncomfortable, tests that God permits in our lives to help strengthen us. But as we keep our gaze straight ahead of us and press toward the prize that God wants for us, we will show ourselves to be more than conquerors through Christ (Romans 8:37).

Personal Reflection

How can you begin to believe and live by God's Word more than you believe and live according to your thoughts and/or feelings?

_____

_____

_____

_____

_____

_____

Letting Go of Guilt and Moving toward Righteousness

Once we decide to take the Lord's advice and give up guilt, shame, and condemnation, we can press toward the understanding Paul desired, which was for us to deeply understand and possess the righteousness of God in Christ and receive it for ourselves as a gift of God's grace. The enemy always seeks to make us feel bad about ourselves, but God justifies us (sees us as though we had never sinned because of Jesus' sacrifice for us on the cross) and reconciles us with Him the moment we are born again, so that, in Him, we no longer have to feel condemned ourselves (2 Corinthians 5:21).

Notice that I make the point that we can feel right about ourselves "in Him." Who we are in Christ is very different from who we are in ourselves. If I look at myself without Jesus, I am wretched, sin-filled, and miserable. But "in Christ," all of us are everything He is through our faith in Him. We are co-heirs with Jesus Christ (Romans 8:17). The apostle John wrote that as Jesus is, "so are we in this world" (1 John 4:17 AMPC).

We Need Spiritual Growth

Just as babies need to grow physically, people who are young in Christ need to grow spiritually. One way God helps us do that is by convicting us of sin or ungodly behavior. But in order for that conviction to help us, we must receive it without allowing it to condemn us or make us feel guilty. I believe that requires us to have a deep and intimate knowledge of God's love for us.

The writer of Hebrews tells his audience that there are many things he would like to tell them, but he cannot. They still need milk, he says, because they are too immature for the meat of the Word. The milk of the Word may be things that encourage us, but the meat of the Word often corrects us. Then he cites the reason they are still spiritually immature, even though by now they should be teaching others. Hebrews 5:13 says, "Anyone who lives on milk, being still an infant, is not acquainted with the teaching about righteousness."

In order to grow out of the baby stage of Christianity, in which young believers are still walking according to the flesh (feelings, thoughts, their own will), we will need to receive correction from God. Correction is good, not bad. I am thankful that God loves us too much to leave us in the condition we are in. His correction comes through His Word, through the Holy Spirit, and through our experiences in life. He always desires to help us move forward, and in order for us to do so, we must face the truth that God shows us about where we are. For example, if God convicts me or shows me in some way that I am greedy or selfish, then I need to receive this correction graciously and let that truth help me improve. But if I am unskilled in the doctrine of righteousness or don't know who I am in Christ, I won't receive the correction. It will only make me feel guilty or bad about myself. Correction is really direction. It is not so much God's showing us what we are doing wrong as showing us what we can do right. His purpose in doing so is to help us enjoy our lives more and, of course, to help us be better ambassadors for Him in the world.

What Does It Mean to Be "in Christ"?

Many people don't understand or have never heard the phrase "who I am in Christ." As we read the Bible, we can find many verses that help us understand who we are in Christ, through faith in Him. When we understand the Bible's teaching about our identity in Christ, we are confident that our value is based on the truth that He loves us and not on what we do. Here are just a few of the many scriptures that offer insight into who we are in Christ.

God made him who had no sin to be sin for us, so that
in him we might become the righteousness of God.

2 Corinthians 5:21, emphasis mine

Praise be to the God and Father of our Lord Jesus
Christ, who has blessed us in the heavenly realms with
every spiritual blessing *in Christ.*

Ephesians 1:3, emphasis mine

And God raised us up with Christ and seated us with
him in the heavenly realms *in Christ Jesus.*

Ephesians 2:6, emphasis mine

Rejoice always, pray continually, give thanks in all circumstances; for this is God's will for you *in Christ Jesus.*

1 Thessalonians 5:16–18, emphasis mine

These scriptures and others like them help teach us who
we are in Christ and what we have in Him. As we live by
the knowledge of our true identity, our lives are changed. I
encourage you to let go of things that are behind you and
press toward what God has ahead for you. Keep learning who
you are in Christ—how valuable, talented, strong, wise, and
hundreds of other qualities that describe you in and through
your relationship with God through Christ.

To be "in Christ" means that we should identify with Him
rather than with what the world says we are. We are new
creatures in Him (2 Corinthians 5:17). Everything old has

passed away and all things have become new. We are strong in Him, redeemed in Him, righteous in Him, valued in Him, and loved in Him.

Once you receive your new identity by faith in Christ, you will begin to behave accordingly. You may have previously believed you were weak and powerless, but once you see that you are strong, you will respond to life's challenges with strength. You may have believed that you were a failure, but when you accept who you are in Christ, you will see that you are moving toward a blessed and successful life. I consider this one of the most important lessons to learn. It is vital for victorious living.

Personal Reflection

What do you need to let go of and leave behind in order to move toward a deeper understanding of who you are in Christ?

_____

_____

_____

_____

_____

_____

Follow the Right Example

Philippians 3:17–21

*Join together in following my example, brothers and sisters,
and just as you have us as a model, keep your eyes on those
who live as we do. For, as I have often told you before and
now tell you again even with tears, many live as enemies
of the cross of Christ. Their destiny is destruction, their
god is their stomach, and their glory is in their shame.
Their mind is set on earthly things. But our citizenship is
in heaven. And we eagerly await a Savior from there, the
Lord Jesus Christ, who, by the power that enables him to
bring everything under his control, will transform our lowly
bodies so that they will be like his glorious body.*

Paul surely must have had confidence in Christ, because he
tells the Philippians to follow his example, that he is a model for
them, and that they could feel safe in following others like him.

Which one of us would have the confidence to say to people: "Model your life after me, and you will be doing the right
thing." I doubt if there are many who would, and possibly not
many who should. It is easier to tell people what they should
do than to show them what to do by example. Words are
always easier than actions.

Paul writes that some people "live as enemies of the cross"

and that destruction is their destiny. There have always been those people who don't believe in God or accept Jesus, but today it seems there are many people who truly behave as enemies of Christ. They are actively working to get God out of everything. They want Him out of our schools, out of government, and out of society altogether. It is interesting that Paul dealt with similar opposition, even in his day.

God will always have enemies, as will those who believe in Him. Our enemies may come against us one way, but they will flee before us seven ways (Deuteronomy 28:7).

I shudder when I think about the condition the enemies of God will find themselves in when they stand before His judgment seat. It seems to me that the most terrible mistake anyone could possibly make is to aggressively come against God and work to remove Him or turn people against Him. The Bible includes many scriptures declaring that the wicked will be destroyed in the end. Here are two examples:

> But all sinners will be destroyed; there will be no future for the wicked.
>
> Psalm 37:38

> He will repay them for their sins and destroy them for their wickedness; the Lord our God will destroy them.
>
> Psalm 94:23

Thankfully, those of us who believe in Christ not only are citizens of the countries we live in, but, even better, we are citizens of heaven. And we wait for the return of Christ, who will take us and those who have died in Him to our heavenly home. We will all receive glorified bodies, which will be like His (Philippians 3:20–21). Just imagine a body that doesn't experience pain or have cellulite, is never sick, and doesn't tempt us to do things that will be harmful to us. I think of having a body that doesn't hinder me in any way, and I must tell you that I get excited! We can only imagine the atmosphere of heaven. We will have total peace, joy, love, and unity. We will not be jealous, angry, insecure, or afraid. We wrestle with many things in this world, but thankfully none of them will exist in heaven.

Let these truths encourage you to hold on to God, no matter how difficult your road in life may be. This lifetime is like one grain of sand in the ocean compared to eternity. One lifetime of even one hundred years is like the blink of an eye compared to forever and ever and ever. Use your time here to prepare for eternal life in heaven. Pay more attention to your spiritual life than to your carnal one, because the day is approaching when this heaven and earth will pass away. But we have a promise that is worth waiting for:

> Then I saw "a new heaven and a new earth," for the first heaven and the first earth had passed away, and there was no longer any sea. I saw the Holy City, the new Jerusalem, coming down out of heaven from God, prepared as a bride beautifully dressed for her husband. And I heard a loud voice from the throne saying, "Look!

God's dwelling place is now among the people, and he will dwell with them. They will be his people, and God himself will be with them and be their God. 'He will wipe every tear from their eyes. There will be no more death' or mourning or crying or pain, for the old order of things has passed away."

Revelation 21:1–4

Personal Reflection

How can you better use your time on earth to prepare for the eternity God has prepared for you?

_____

_____

_____

_____

_____

_____

_____

CHAPTER 13

STAND FIRM, STAY UNITED, AND BE AT PEACE

Enjoy Peace

Philippians 4:1–3

Therefore, my brothers and sisters, you whom I love and long for, my joy and crown, stand firm in the Lord in this way, dear friends! I plead with Euodia and I plead with Syntyche to be of the same mind in the Lord. Yes, and I ask you, my true companion, help these women since they have contended at my side in the cause of the gospel, along with Clement and the rest of my co-workers, whose names are in the book of life.

Paul had a deep, affectionate love for the people to whom he ministered, and he calls the Philippians his "joy and crown." He urges them to stand firm. This is something we all need to be encouraged to do. Life is not usually easy, and very few people get through it without experiencing some deep pain and disappointment. Thankfully, we don't just have trouble at times; we always have Jesus, who helps and comforts us in our troubles.

We would be wise to remember that we have an enemy, Satan, who continually seeks opportunities to attack us in various ways. Many of these attacks are against our mind. The enemy always tells us our troubles will never end, but they always do, because greater is He who is in us than he who is in the world (1 John 4:4). We don't need to fear the enemy; we simply need to be ready to stand firm and determine never to give up. Then we will see God move on our behalf. Victory is already ours, even though we may need to be patient for a while.

Personal Reflection

In what ways do you need to stand firm against the enemy right now?

_____

_____

_____

_____

_____

_____

Aim for Unity

Next, Paul moves to a subject he mentions repeatedly: the importance of unity. There were two women, Euodia and Syntyche, in the Philippian church who had worked diligently by Paul's side for the cause of the gospel, but they were no longer unified; there was strife between them. Paul urges them "to be of the same mind in the Lord." I admit that I think Paul's instruction is a big challenge. We all are so different, and all too often we do not think alike. However, Paul urges us to press past our own ideas and work for what keeps us unified. We can disagree, but we can also learn to disagree agreeably.

Most of the things people disagree about and end up in heated arguments about are, in the end, unimportant. I recall a time when I was in a heated argument with Dave about which route he should take to the hardware store. As we argued, vying for the position of "being right," the Lord spoke to my heart and said, "What difference does it make in spreading the gospel which way Dave drives to the store?" I saw how ridiculous we were both being, and I quit arguing and simply enjoyed the ride. The best way to enjoy life is to let the man drive and don't give him advice about how to do it!

No two people will ever think alike on absolutely everything, but if both have the humble mind Paul writes about in Philippians 2, even if they don't agree, they will respect one another's viewpoint and work for peace and unity, because this pleases God. Peace and unity do not come easily. Achieving them takes a strong commitment from each of us to resist strife, taking offense, unforgiveness, bitterness, and resentment.

We should learn how to choose our battles wisely if we want to maintain peace and unity. Most things are simply not worth the emotional energy required to argue about them. Paul not only encouraged the two women directly, but he also urged others to help them get along. We should do the same with people we know. We should be peacemakers!

At Joyce Meyer Ministries, we work to maintain unity, which often requires dealing with issues between people that need to be talked out. One of our pastors oversees conflict resolution. He works as an arbitrator between the offended parties, helping them come to a godly resolution. The value of unity in our organization is well worth the effort we invest in keeping it.

Peace, Joy, and Gentleness

Philippians 4:4–5

Rejoice in the Lord always. I will say it again: Rejoice! Let your gentleness be evident to all. The Lord is near.

These verses are packed full of helpful instructions for our daily lives. As we know, Philippians is the epistle of joy. In Philippians 4:4, Paul not only says once that we are to rejoice, but he repeats this instruction. Joy and rejoicing must have been very important to Paul, and he obviously felt they are also important for every believer.

Personal Reflection

What are some reasons you can rejoice today?

_____

_____

_____

_____

_____

The word translated *gentleness* in Philippians 4:5 (NIV) is translated using different words in other versions of the Bible. Some of the words used are *reasonableness* (ESV), *moderation* (KJV), *considerateness* and *forbearing spirit* (AMPC). Paul is saying that we are to let our sweet, forbearing, gentle spirits be known to everyone, even when we face challenges. In fact, I believe the most important time for us to demonstrate these good qualities and display the fruit of the Holy Spirit (Galatians 5:22–23) is during difficulty. If we behave with gentleness only when our lives are going well, we are no different than those who do not believe in Jesus Christ. Anyone can be gentle and reasonable when they have nothing pressing against them, but only those who belong to Christ can, by the Holy Spirit, have consistent godly behavior.

What does Paul's statement "the Lord is near" mean? Does it mean we should watch our behavior because Jesus' return is close at hand? It may mean that, but I think we should also consider that it could mean we should manifest these godly qualities because the Lord is always standing by. He is always with us; He sees every action we take and hears every word we speak. Hebrews 4:13 says, "Nothing in all creation is hidden from God's sight. Everything is uncovered and laid bare before the eyes of him to whom we must give account."

We are comforted by the thought that God will never leave

us or forsake us and that He will be with us always, but we may not have considered that this fact also means He sees and knows everything we do. Let us choose to live for God's pleasure, with the help of the Holy Spirit, simply because we love Him.

Be Anxious for Nothing

Philippians 4:6–7

*Do not be anxious about anything, but in every situation,
by prayer and petition, with thanksgiving, present your
requests to God. And the peace of God, which transcends
all understanding, will guard your hearts and your minds
in Christ Jesus.*

In Philippians 4:6–7 we find four practical and powerful
principles: Don't worry. Pray. Be thankful. Enjoy peace. I
can't tell you how often I meditate on or declare these scriptures, especially if the enemy is tempting me to worry.

Most of us have ample opportunity to worry and be anxious daily, but we have other options. We can pray about
what we need or want. We can pray about the situations that
concern us, and through prayer we can invite God to work in
those circumstances. While we are presenting our petitions
to God, we are to live lives of gratitude and thanksgiving. No
matter how many problems we might have, each of us has
more blessings than difficulties. If we are ungrateful for what
we already have, why should God give us more? Wouldn't
we merely have more to complain about? We may think we

would be happy and grateful if only we didn't have just one certain problem. But experience tells us that unless we have thankful hearts that always look for reasons to be grateful, we will always find something to complain about, no matter what God does for us.

Paul assures us that if we refuse to be anxious and if we pray and give thanks, God's peace will be ours, and it will guard our hearts in a way that transcends all understanding. Being content or discontent has very little to do with our circumstances but everything to do with our heart toward God.

If you want some practical tips on avoiding worry, I suggest replacing "worry thoughts" with thoughts about times you have had problems and God has helped you. Godly thoughts will strengthen your faith. Another suggestion is to get your mind off of your problem by doing something other than thinking about it and talking about it continually. Go do something. Get involved in helping someone else who is hurting. Have lunch or coffee with a friend. If you are occupied with something other than your problem, it won't take a front row seat in your mind.

Personal Reflection

To what specific situations in your life do you need to apply the four principles of Philippians 4:6–7 (don't worry; pray; be thankful; enjoy peace)?

_____

_____

_____

_____

_____

_____

_____

Worry seems to be the national pastime. Some people even believe it is their duty to worry about their children when they are out with their friends, but praying for God to grant them wisdom and protect them would be a much better use of their time. I was once a chief worrier, and it took me quite a while to have a breakthrough in this area. I worried until I finally realized that I just simply wasn't intelligent enough to solve my own problems and that I needed God's help. The way to get God's help is through prayer (asking) and living with an attitude of gratitude while you are waiting for the breakthrough you need.

Worry is useless. It has many negative side effects and no positive ones. It can give us headaches, stress, tension, fear, negative attitudes, stomach problems, sleepless nights, and many other miseries. It is like rocking in a rocking chair in that it keeps us busy but gets us nowhere.

If you have struggled with worry, as I have, let me encourage you that your experience with God's faithfulness will help immensely. Each time you see God solve a problem for you and remember it, your faith will gain strength. Consider keeping a gratitude journal in which you record times when you have seen God help you and bring you victory.

When you are under an attack of worry, instead of wrestling against the worry and trying very hard not to worry, invite God into your situation. Ask the Holy Spirit to help you then hold your peace while God works in your situation.

CHAPTER 14

THE BELIEVER'S MINDSET, THE POWER OF CONTENTMENT, AND THE SOURCE OF OUR STRENGTH

Think about These Things

Philippians 4:8–9

*Finally, brothers and sisters, whatever is true, whatever
is noble, whatever is right, whatever is pure, whatever is
lovely, whatever is admirable—if anything is excellent or
praiseworthy—think about such things. Whatever you
have learned or received or heard from me, or seen in
me—put it into practice. And the God of peace will be
with you.*

While we are waiting for answers to our prayers and for
the help we need from God to deal with our difficulties in
life, we think about many things. What we think about can
either upset us more or help us remain peaceful in the storm.
Whatever we think about determines what our lives will be.
Happy thoughts produce a happy life. Paul lists seven qualities of things we should think about. Although there are others, these certainly give us a great place to start:

- **True:** If we think and talk about our circumstances,
  we may be thinking and talking about the facts in our
  lives at the current time, but Jesus promises that the
  truth will set us free (John 8:32). Truth is greater than
  facts, and it can ultimately change them. We may

have a problem to which we don't have an answer, and that is the fact, but the truth is that God does know the answer. He loves us and will never leave us helpless. He is our Deliverer, and He is faithful. Keep lifting up the truth of God's Word and let it work against any facts that don't agree with it.

- **Noble:** A simple definition I like to use for the Greek word for *noble* is having or showing fine personality qualities and high moral character. We can also think of being noble as being an excellent person. Let us think on excellent things—what God has done for us, what we can do for other people in need, ways we can spread the gospel, how we can live a life that glorifies God, and so on. There are so many noble and honorable things to meditate on; why fix our minds on low and base things or things that are negative? God sets before us death and life, good and evil, and urges us to choose life and good things (Deuteronomy 30:19).

- **Right:** To be right means to be just, fair minded, unbiased, impartial, and unprejudiced. God is just. He always does what is right, and He is impartial. When we have a situation that is unjust and painful to us, we can trust God to bring justice on our behalf. He takes our ashes and gives us His beauty (Isaiah 61:3). God takes bad things and turns them into good things. We should enjoy God's justice in our lives, and we should also strive to be just in our dealings with other people.

- **Pure:** The Greek word used here for *pure* means clean. Let us have clean thoughts, thoughts that Jesus would think, rather than thoughts the flesh or the world thinks. Jesus said that the pure in heart are blessed, for they shall see God (Matthew 5:8). I believe this refers to the ability of the pure in heart to hear clearly from God and to be more aware of His presence, as well as seeing Him face-to-face when we are taken to our heavenly home.
- **Lovely:** The Greek word used here for *lovely* means pleasing and agreeable. Our thoughts should be agreeable with God's Word, and when they are, they will be pleasing to God. To develop the habit of meditating on His Word is one of the best things we can do.
- **Admirable:** When we think of people we know, we should think of their strengths and abilities, the qualities we admire about them. Think about the things that make them good examples for others. Everyone has weaknesses we can choose to focus on, but they also have strengths upon which we can focus. The decision is up to us, but if we desire joy, we should always focus on good things.
- **Excellent and praiseworthy:** We need to think on matters that are good and excellent. We should think on the best aspects of God and the best things in our lives. We can think of all the good that God does and of the people who are blessings in our lives. We can think positively and have thoughts filled with hope.

We can also think of plenty of things for which to
praise God, and anything that we can think of that
gives us a reason to give praise to God is always a
good thing to have on our minds.

Our thoughts become our words, and thoughts and words
both affect our moods. Our thoughts, words, and emotions
come together and influence our actions, so we can see that
in many ways our thoughts ultimately become our lives. Perhaps we should ask ourselves if we want to have the things
we have been thinking about, and if not, then make a change
for the better.

Personal Reflection

Take a moment to consider a specific circumstance
in your life. How could you think about it in ways that
are true, noble, right, pure, lovely, admirable, excellent, and praiseworthy?

_____

_____

_____

_____

_____

Contentment

Philippians 4:10–13

I rejoiced greatly in the Lord that at last you renewed your concern for me. Indeed, you were concerned, but you had no opportunity to show it. I am not saying this because I am in need, for I have learned to be content whatever the circumstances. I know what it is to be in need, and I know what it is to have plenty. I have learned the secret of being content in any and every situation, whether well fed or hungry, whether living in plenty or in want. I can do all this through him who gives me strength.

Philippians 4:10–13 contains several important messages for all believers. Paul speaks of contentment and of God's ability and desire to meet all of our needs, and he informs us that we can do all things through the strength of Christ.

Paul rejoices greatly that the Lord has caused the Philippians to be concerned for his welfare and respond to him in practical ways that would benefit and help him. It is always good when we pray for someone, but in certain situations, we need to add some practical benefit to our prayers.

Paul had sown spiritually into the lives of the Philippian believers, and they wanted to give back by meeting some of his physical needs. They had been concerned all along and wanted to do something, but this was their first opportunity. We should take advantage of the opportunities God gives us to help and bless others. Paul wrote to the Galatians that they should bless others as opportunities came to them (Galatians 6:10). Let's determine not to miss a single chance that God gives us to be a blessing to someone else.

We may mistakenly think that our joy comes from getting something we want, but the truth is that we get more joy from giving than we do from getting. "It is more blessed to give than to receive" (Acts 20:35).

Paul knew what it was to be in need and to have plenty, and he had learned to be content either way. Contentment is a wonderful quality to have. We can want something without letting the desire for it cause us to be discontent with what we have right now, and we are to give thanks in *all* circumstances (1 Thessalonians 5:18).

Personal Reflection

What is a situation in which you need to grow in contentment in your life?

_____

_____

_____

_____

I Can Do All Things

Paul goes on to say in Philippians 4:13 that it is God who gives him the strength to be content and to do everything else he does, according to God's will. This is another scripture we often hear quoted and taken out of context. The truth is that we can do what God gives us to do, not merely anything we decide to do. God gave Paul the strength to have plenty or to be hungry—and to be content either way. I believe God desires that we all grow spiritually to the point where we can be as content as Paul was. I think our contentment gives God glory.

We can be assured that God will always give us "grace for our place." Whatever He assigns to us, we can do it through His strength. But this does not mean that we can do anything we choose.

I took this scripture out of context in my life for a period of time, and I worked too hard, thinking, *I can do all things through Christ.* But I was actually just trying to make something happen that I wanted to happen, and I was disobeying God's laws of rest. He will give me strength to obey Him, but He will not give me grace and strength to disobey Him.

When God asks us to do something difficult, we need never say, "I can't do that; it's too hard," because God strengthens us for what He calls us to do. If you are raising a special needs child, God will give you the strength to do it. If you are struggling with financial lack, God will show you ways to economize or ways you can earn extra income. Whatever your circumstances, God will never leave you helpless.

Personal Reflection

In what areas of your life do you need God to strengthen you right now? Will you choose to believe He will give you grace for your place?

_____

_____

_____

_____

_____

Be Committed

Philippians 4:14–20

Yet it was good of you to share in my troubles. Moreover,
as you Philippians know, in the early days of your
acquaintance with the gospel, when I set out from
Macedonia, not one church shared with me in the matter
of giving and receiving, except you only; for even when I
was in Thessalonica, you sent me aid more than once when
I was in need. Not that I desire your gifts; what I desire
is that more be credited to your account. I have received
full payment and have more than enough. I am amply
supplied, now that I have received from Epaphroditus the
gifts you sent. They are a fragrant offering, an acceptable
sacrifice, pleasing to God. And my God will meet all your
needs according to the riches of his glory in Christ Jesus.
To our God and Father be glory for ever and ever. Amen.

Paul mentions that in the early days of his ministry, the Philippians were the only church that partnered with him in spreading the gospel. And in addition, the Philippians were committed to continuing to support him. The Amplified Bible, Classic Edition says they were the only church who opened "a debit and credit account" with Paul (Philippians 4:15 AMPC). I like that thought because it gives insight into how we should view the people who minister to us. Paul was putting something into their account, and they responded by putting into his account resources that would enable him to continue ministering to them and others. We should be as committed to our ministers as we expect them to be to us. Let's be diligent not to allow ourselves to fall into the trap of being "takers." We should always respond by giving and blessing those who give to and bless us.

Paul is clear that he is not seeking their money (gift), but that he was seeking the credit that would accrue to their account in heaven.

Then he makes them a promise, saying, "God will meet all your needs according to the riches of his glory in Christ Jesus" (Philippians 4:19). For many years I heard this promise quoted and preached about without hearing what the Philippians did, which was to bless Paul. God promises us many things, and He is always faithful. But we also have a responsibility to obey God in doing our part.

There are times when God does miracles and provides for us in amazing ways. Whether He does it through a miracle or by leading us to take some type of action, God will provide! And as Paul writes in Philippians 4:20, we should always give God glory, knowing He will provide for us as we trust in His goodness and wisdom.

Final Greetings and Prayer

Philippians 4:21–23

Greet all God's people in Christ Jesus. The brothers and sisters who are with me send greetings. All God's people here send you greetings, especially those who belong to Caesar's household. The grace of the Lord Jesus Christ be with your spirit. Amen.

Paul closes his epistle to the Philippians by sending greetings to fellow believers and sharing greetings from those who were with him. He finishes the letter similarly to the way he began it, praying for the Philippians to know the grace of Jesus Christ. As I mentioned in chapter 1, that is a very powerful prayer.

IN CLOSING

Remember, Paul wrote letters to various churches because he was unable to visit them as often as he would have liked to have been with them in person. His letters are extremely valuable and should be studied carefully. They remind us not only of who we are in Christ but also of how we should respond to all that God has done for us and what kind of life we should live considering it.

I want to remind you again that Paul's epistle to the Philippians is considered the epistle of joy, and that joy gives us strength. You have probably noticed as you have read this book how often Paul mentions joy, and I hope the level of joy in your life will increase as a result of studying Philippians.

Paul also writes quite a bit about unity and the importance of our thoughts in his letter to the Philippians. Both unity and thinking according to God's Word are vital to believers today.

H. A. Ironside summarizes the four chapters in Philippians in his *Notes on the Epistle to the Philippians* like this, and I have added my own observations to his:

In Philippians 1, we see Christ as "the believer's life," and we realize the importance of living with a single mind.

In Philippians 2, we see Christ as "the believer's example," and we recognize the importance of having a humble mind.

In Philippians 3, we see Christ as "the believer's goal," our reason for living, and we come to understand the importance of having a spiritual and determined mind.

And, in Philippians 4 we see Christ as "the believer's strength" and source, and we learn about the importance of having a confident and secure mind.

If we can see Christ as Ironside indicates in these four points, we will experience powerful growth in our relationship with Him.

Paul's letter to the Philippians deserves frequent study, and I pray that this book about this epistle has helped you greatly.

Do you have a real relationship with Jesus?

God loves you! He created you to be a special, unique, one-of-a-kind individual, and He has a specific purpose and plan for your life. And through a personal relationship with your Creator—God—you can discover a way of life that will truly satisfy your soul.

No matter who you are, what you've done, or where you are in your life right now, God's love and grace are greater than your sin—your mistakes. Jesus willingly gave His life so you can receive forgiveness from God and have new life in Him. He's just waiting for you to invite Him to be your Savior and Lord.

If you are ready to commit your life to Jesus and follow Him, all you have to do is ask Him to forgive your sins and give you a fresh start in the life you are meant to live. Begin by praying this prayer...

Lord Jesus, thank You for giving Your life for me and forgiving me of my sins so I can have a personal relationship with You. I am sincerely sorry for the mistakes I've made, and I know I need You to help me live right.

Your Word says in Romans 10:9, "If you declare with your mouth, 'Jesus is Lord,' and believe in your heart that God raised him from the dead, you will be saved" (NIV). I believe You are the Son of God and confess You as my Savior and Lord. Take me just as I am, and work in my heart, making me the person You want me to be. I want to live for You, Jesus, and I am so grateful that You are giving me a fresh start in my new life with You today.

I love You, Jesus!

It's so amazing to know that God loves us so much! He wants to have a deep, intimate relationship with us that grows every day as we spend time with Him in prayer and Bible study. And we want to encourage you in your new life in Christ.

Please visit **joycemeyer.org/knowJesus** to request Joyce's book *A New Way of Living*, which is our gift to you. We also have other free resources online to help you make progress in pursuing everything God has for you.

Congratulations on your fresh start in your life in Christ! We hope to hear from you soon.

Joyce Meyer is one of the world's leading practical Bible teachers. A *New York Times* bestselling author, Joyce's books have helped millions of people find hope and restoration through Jesus Christ. Joyce's program *Enjoying Everyday Life* airs around the world on television, radio, and the Internet. Through Joyce Meyer Ministries, Joyce teaches internationally on a number of topics with a particular focus on how the Word of God applies to our everyday lives. Her candid communication style allows her to share openly and practically about her experiences so others can apply what she has learned to their lives.

Joyce has authored more than one hundred books, which have been translated into more than one hundred languages, and over 65 million of her books have been distributed worldwide. Bestsellers include *Power Thoughts*; *The Confident Woman*; *Look Great, Feel Great*; *Starting Your Day Right*; *Ending Your Day Right*; *Approval Addiction*; *How to Hear from God*; *Beauty for Ashes*; and *Battlefield of the Mind*.

Joyce's passion to help hurting people is foundational to the vision of Hand of Hope, the missions arm of Joyce Meyer

Ministries. Hand of Hope provides worldwide humanitarian outreaches such as feeding programs, medical care, orphanages, disaster response, human trafficking intervention and rehabilitation, and much more—always sharing the love and Gospel of Christ.

JOYCE MEYER MINISTRIES

U.S. & FOREIGN OFFICE ADDRESSES

Joyce Meyer Ministries
P.O. Box 655
Fenton, MO 63026
USA
(636) 349-0303

Joyce Meyer Ministries—
Canada
P.O. Box 7700
Vancouver, BC V6B 4E2
Canada
(800) 868-1002

Joyce Meyer Ministries—
Australia
Locked Bag 77
Mansfield Delivery Centre
Queensland 4122
Australia
(07) 3349 1200

Joyce Meyer Ministries—
England
P.O. Box 1549
Windsor SL4 1GT
United Kingdom
01753 831102

Joyce Meyer Ministries—
South Africa
P.O. Box 5
Cape Town 8000
South Africa
(27) 21-701-1056

Joyce Meyer Ministries—
Francophonie
29 avenue Maurice Chevalier
77330 Ozoir la Ferriere
France

Joyce Meyer Ministries—
Germany
Postfach 761001
22060 Hamburg
Germany
+49 (0)40 / 88 88 4 11 11

Joyce Meyer Ministries—
Netherlands
Lorenzlaan 14
7002 HB Doetinchem
+31 657 555 9789

Joyce Meyer Ministries—
Russia
P.O. Box 789
Moscow 101000
Russia
+7 (495) 727-14-68

Other Books by Joyce Meyer

Overload

The Penny

Perfect Love (previously published as *God Is Not Mad at You*)*

The Power of Being Positive

The Power of Being Thankful

The Power of Determination

The Power of Forgiveness

The Power of Simple Prayer

Power Thoughts

Power Thoughts Devotional

Quiet Times with God Devotional

Reduce Me to Love

The Secret Power of Speaking God's Word

The Secrets of Spiritual Power

The Secret to True Happiness

Seven Things That Steal Your Joy

Start Your New Life Today

Starting Your Day Right

Straight Talk

Teenagers Are People Too!

Trusting God Day by Day

The Word, the Name, the Blood

Woman to Woman

You Can Begin Again

*Your Battles Belong to the Lord**

Joyce Meyer Spanish Titles

Belleza en Lugar de Cenizas (*Beauty for Ashes*)

Buena Salud, Buena Vida (*Good Health, Good Life*)

Cambia Tus Palabras, Cambia Tu Vida (*Change Your Words, Change Your Life*)

El Campo de Batalla de la Mente (Battlefield of the Mind)

Como Formar Buenos Habitos y Romper Malos Habitos (Making Good Habits, Breaking Bad Habits)

La Conexión de la Mente (The Mind Connection)

Dios No Está Enojado Contigo (God Is Not Mad at You)

La Dosis de Aprobación (The Approval Fix)

Efesios: Comentario Biblico (Ephesians: Biblical Commentary)

Empezando Tu Día Bien (Starting Your Day Right)

Hágalo con Miedo (Do It Afraid)

Hazte un Favor a Ti Mismo...Perdona (Do Yourself a Favor...Forgive)

Madre Segura de Sí Misma (The Confident Mom)

Momentos de Quietud con Dios (Quiet Times with God Devotional)

Pensamientos de Poder (Power Thoughts)

Sanidad para el Alma de Una Mujer (Healing the Soul of a Woman)

Santiago: Comentario Bíblico (James: Biblical Commentary)

Sobrecarga (Overload)*

Sus Batallas Son del Señor (Your Battles Belong to the Lord)

Termina Bien tu Día (Ending Your Day Right)

Usted Puede Comenzar de Nuevo (You Can Begin Again)

Viva Valientemente (Living Courageously)

* Study Guide available for this title

Books by Dave Meyer

Life Lines